Advance Praise for *Moving to Great*

"Eric has a unique enthusiasm and charisma that sets him apart, and you could always tell he was going to be a great success in life. *Moving to Great* does a phenomenal job of capturing the essence of his passion in really special ways."

—PETE CARROLL, HEAD COACH AND EXECUTIVE VICE PRESIDENT, SEATTLE SEAHAWKS

"Eric's coaching transforms leaders and organizations by truly moving people toward their greatest potential. He delivered tangible results for me and my team, helping us to lead better and live better. Eric is amazing, and so is *Moving to Great!*"

—WENDY COLLIE, CEO, NEW SEASONS MARKET

"Eric's encouragement and insight created a competitive advantage for me and my team of more than seven thousand managers. Now these same insights that helped us unleash our potential are available in the pages of *Moving to Great.*"

—JIM ALLING, CEO, TOMS SHOES

"*Moving to Great* is simple, useful, and powerful truth. I can see Eric's many years of experience coaching leaders and helping organizations navigate change reflected in the pages of this book."

—CHRISTINE DEPUTY, CHRO, EVP HUMAN RESOURCES, NORDSTROM

"I have worked with Eric for almost twenty years, in three different companies. Every time, he has delivered tangible results. I highly recommend *Moving to Great.*"

—PAUL TWOHIG, PRESIDENT, DUNKIN' DONUTS

"Eric Boles is the real deal. I've been his friend for twenty-five years and can tell you...he walks the walk. His counsel, training, and guidance have been the single most influential factor, outside the Bible, in developing my leadership style and philosophy—both as an NFL quarterback in incredibly diverse locker rooms and now as a head football coach at the high school level."

—JON KITNA, FOOTBALL COACH AND FORMER NFL QUARTERBACK

"Eric is a tremendous coach and leader. For almost twenty years, he has helped me dramatically increase my effectiveness. His ideas and principles change businesses and change lives. You and your team need *Moving to Great!*"

—WELDON SPANGLER, SVP, BASKIN-ROBBINS

"Eric helps people see their potential for greatness, and his simple, straightforward, and engaging approach inspires people to action. In *Moving to Great,* Eric points the way from possibility to reality, a reality I've seen him create in teams across multiple continents, cultures, and organizations over the last decade. Eric has changed many lives…including my own."

—RICH NELSEN, CEO, IN-SHAPE HEALTH CLUBS

"I love Eric Boles, and you will too! *Moving to Great* is an exciting process of personal exploration and continuous improvement. It is motivating, inspiring, and thought provoking. The principles Eric shares within this book are true life lessons that apply far beyond business."

—JOHN DAWSON, CHIEF DEVELOPMENT OFFICER, EL POLLO LOCO

MOVING TO
GREAT

Unleashing Your Best in Life and Work

ERIC BOLES

STONE
LOUNGE

New York

Moving to Great

Copyright © 2017 Eric Boles

Published by Stone Lounge Press, New York

ISBN: 978-1-945556-01-2

Book Design: Carla Green
Editing: Bruce Nygren

Special discounts are available on quantity purchases by corporations, associations, and others. For details, and to order additional copies of this book, please visit www.TheGameChangersInc.com or www.StoneLoungePress.com.

Publisher's Cataloging-in-Publication data

Boles, Eric, 1970- author.
Moving to great: unleashing your best in life and work / by Eric Boles
192 pages   cm
ISBN 978-1-945556-01-2 (hardcover)

1. Self-actualization (Psychology) 2. Self-perception.
3. Goal (Psychology) 4. Achievement motivation. 5. Success.
6. Self-help techniques. 7. Self-help publications.   I. Title.

BF637.S4B6555 2017   158.1
QBI17-900016

First Edition
Printed in the United States of America
2 4 6 8 10 9 7 5 3 1

CONTENTS

INTRODUCTION

I didn't know. After two attempts to answer his question, the shallowness sunk in. When he asked me a third time, I realized my heart and mind were blank. I had nothing. His eyes pierced my soul as he walked away.

What just happened?

I had been answering this question with ease my entire life, but in that moment the discomfort paralyzed me. I stood there in disbelief as I replayed the conversation over and over in my head.

"Eric, who are you?"

"I'm Eric Boles."

"I didn't ask your name. I asked, 'Who are you?'"

"I'm a wide receiver for the New York Jets."

"I didn't ask what you do. I asked, 'Who are you?'"

His voice echoed in my mind for hours. I was twenty-three years old and didn't have a clue who I was beyond my job description. I didn't know what I stood for, and I didn't know what mattered to me. I had a lot to learn.

Today, many years later, I am an inspired practitioner of the Moving to Great (MTG) philosophy that begins with that very same question. It is a journey that begins with awareness, and it begins with who you are.

Like a football game, MTG is divided into four quarters, and your goal is to win every quarter. The first quarter addresses the question of, "Who am I?" The second quarter uncovers, "How did I get here?"

Now it's halftime. During the first half, we started strong and in the second half, we will finish strong.

The third quarter begins with momentum as we explore, "Where am I going?" We close the game in the fourth quarter with, "How do I get there?"

These simple yet significant questions affect your level of awareness and ability to sustain success. As you become more effective as a person and a leader, you will recognize the importance of continually asking yourself these questions to ensure continued success.

The first question involves self-reflection and contemplation. You clarify your identity as you become more aware of your potential, ability to change, and self-imposed limitations.

The second question explores your level of conscious thinking. It addresses your belief system, attitude, self-image, and self-esteem. Your attitude is a game-changer, because it multiplies your results to the infinite degree while your self-esteem is your psychological immune system that offers you resiliency during the challenging times.

You might be surprised, but many people have limited insight with respect to how they got to where they are. If by chance you are one of those people, don't worry—the MTG principles will help you develop this skill.

The third question digs into your values and goal-setting for clarity. It is a process of strategic planning to get as much return on energy as possible. You invest time, money, effort, and creativity in order to get results, and that return on energy propels you to where you want to go.

The fourth question introduces the importance of self-regulation, growing your belief system, and finalizing your personal game plan. It is one thing to have a goal, and it is another thing to *believe* you can attain that goal. You learn how to grow your beliefs so that you can manifest them in your experience and finally turn them into expectations. Your personal game plan brings everything together and incorporates your discoveries as you move through the previous three quarters of *Moving to Great*.

In the fourth quarter, it is now time to take action. I repeat, take action. Remember, nothing changes until something moves. Keep in mind, it is called *Moving to Great* for a reason. There is no such thing as "standing around" for great or "sitting around" for great. You can't create greatness by contemplating it. Only action is action, and MTG is a progression. It is a journey.

Nothing changes until something moves.

What makes *Moving to Great* such a significant game-changer is that the skills and tools provided not only help you personally, but they also help you professionally. It is a true win-win. This creates a unique synergy that collapses time. If you've ever felt this synergy, or been a part of it, there's nothing like it.

My wife, Cindy, and I have individual goals, but when we share a collective shared goal, magic happens. Not only do we grow together during the process, but the results are that much sweeter. That same thing can happen with those around you.

It is time to break through your mental and self-imposed limitations and perform at new and higher levels in all areas of your life.

We live in a new reality where the speed of change has never been faster and more prevalent. Meeting expectations is now associated with mediocrity instead of success, and fear is minimizing your results. As you align yourself with the MTG principles, your perspective and mindset will shift from fear and insecurity to hope and confidence. You will realize that problems are simply disguised opportunities, and the future couldn't be brighter.

Just as I attended training camp back in 1992 for the New York Jets, *Moving to Great* is your training camp, and this is your playbook. Are you ready?

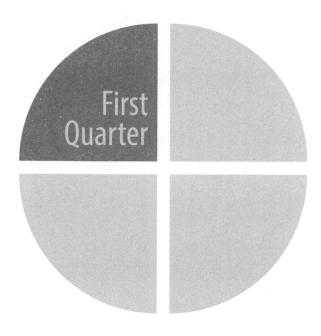

First
Quarter

Who Am I?

UNTAPPED POTENTIAL

Everything I can be, but have not yet become.
Everything I can do, but have not yet done.

A s a child, I wanted to be significant *so* badly. I wanted to matter, and I wanted to be great.

I daydreamed all the time. When I was supposed to be mowing the lawn, I was hitting rocks over the fence and winning the World Series. As I threw things in the garbage, I imagined making the winning basket in the NBA championship game. Instead of raking the leaves, I would dive on the pile as if I just scored the winning touchdown in the Super Bowl.

There was a part of me that wanted to be great and influential.

Can you relate?

Growing up, I was the smallest kid on the team. In seventh grade, I was only 4'11" and weighed 90 pounds. When I was a junior in high school, I was 5'10", but going into my senior year, I grew like a weed. I was almost 6'3"! I looked like a deer—big hands, big feet, and skinny as a rail. I doubt I weighed more than 150 pounds.

Throughout middle school and high school, I played both football and basketball. I know I made the teams every year because one of the assistant coaches liked me. I didn't deserve to be on the teams, but I gave it all my effort. My teammates were the real talented ones. The coaches liked that I was a hard worker.

One day my coach looked at me and said, "Eric, one day you'll see. You will be the finest athlete to ever come out of this school."

Now, you must understand there was no evidence to support what he was saying, but I will never forget that day.

Lo and behold, a few years later, I was a collegiate All-American at Central Washington University and was drafted into the NFL to play wide receiver for the New York Jets. Finally, my opportunity to feel significant was here! I was ready to make a difference. Everything that I wanted most was taking place.

What I didn't know was that despite my natural ability and talent and all of the accolades that I had received in college, I had many mental roadblocks and a self-defeating attitude. As physically talented as I was, sadly, my time in the NFL was less than fulfilled. For me, the NFL not only stood for National Football League, but also Not For Long.

During my first year with the New York Jets, I blew out my right knee. I tore my lateral collateral ligament (LCL). Then in my second year, I tore my calf muscle. Even though these were physical injuries, I was injured mentally as well. I lacked confidence, and I didn't believe that I was good enough to be playing as a pro. I was given an injury settlement, which meant that they paid me to go away.

> *Despite my natural ability and talent and all of the accolades that I had received in college, I had many mental roadblocks and a self-defeating attitude.*

I received another chance when the San Diego Chargers picked me up for half a season, but it ended before it began. The Chargers didn't bother to tell me they were about to release me. I spent half a day in team meetings before realizing that my name wasn't on the depth chart. In a normal business setting, the depth chart would be like the organizational chart.

Have you ever been rejected by someone, yet they didn't tell you? That's what it felt like for me.

After being released from the Chargers, I drove home from San Diego, California, to Tacoma, Washington. I was so discouraged that I didn't call or talk to anybody during the twenty-four-hour trip. As soon as I arrived home, my mother came running out the front door telling me that the Green Bay Packers had been trying to get a hold of me because they wanted to sign me!

So after surviving that excruciating twenty-four-hour drive, the next day turned out to be one of the best days of my life! Shortly thereafter, I found myself in the locker room sitting with some of the greatest football players to ever play the game. Brett Favre, a legendary quarterback, was on my right, and the late Reggie White, one of the greatest defensive players of all time, was on my left. These guys were my teammates. *Could this be my chance, my big break?*

During my time with the Packers, I severely pulled my hamstring and one day was told that the general manager, Ron Wolf, wanted to see me. I assumed that he wanted an update on my injury, but just as I was heading up to his office, I was told to bring my playbook. My heart sank. When a player was asked to see the general manager and bring his playbook, it was over. Sure enough, I got cut, dismissed, and promoted to fan—and it *seemed* like my teammates, the media, and the fans already knew about it. Without having the opportunity to say goodbye to my teammates, I was on my way out of the Packers's locker room, out of Lambeau Field, and out of the NFL. I had to walk out by the same people who had asked me for my autograph on my way in.

Public humiliation.

At the time, I remember sitting with my future wife, Cindy, asking the question, "What am I going to do?" I had no job and no income. At first, I couldn't let go of the NFL. I hoped and prayed that I would eventually get back on a team, but it never happened. I began to question who I was. I had been convinced that the NFL was my path in life. *How could something that I worked so hard for be gone so quickly? Now that it's gone, who am I?*

To make ends meet, I started doing janitorial work—a college-educated, former professional football player cleaning US West buildings at night. One evening when I was cleaning, a gentleman working in his cubicle rolled back in his chair and pointed at the floor, so I walked closer. He was pointing at some dirt beneath his desk. I swept it up and without looking at me or saying anything, he rolled his chair back.

Less than a year earlier, I had felt significant as a professional football player. Now, a man was pointing his finger at me to clean up dirt beneath his desk without feeling the need even to acknowledge me.

This man was likely to have asked for my autograph nine months prior. How did I fall so fast and so hard? What did I do wrong?

Instead of seeing this as temporary, I started to feel like this was my actual life and that my previous high moments were exceptions to the rule. I was angry and depressed. *Why did God give me a taste of what I thought I wanted most to simply yank it away?*

> *How did I fall so fast and so hard? What did I do wrong?*

Six months later, while I was volunteering at a United Way event, one of the guest speakers said something that would in time change my life. His name was Bob Moawad.

I will never forget how his words spoke to the very core of me. He was talking about the importance of attitude and how fear puts a ceiling on your potential and limits what you are capable of doing. He described how peak performers think and how they differ from low performers. He further explained the characteristics of low performers.

My jaw dropped. *He was describing me!* It wasn't until that moment I realized what I was missing. I had believed that because I was physically gifted, everything else would take care of itself. I was dead wrong.

Even though I had heard this advice before, it wasn't until that moment I actually heard it. I had been going to church all my life. I had heard countless athletes speak; I had heard some of the best locker room speeches, but it wasn't until that moment that I realized that I was the one holding the keys to unleash my potential.

In my ignorance, I was violating the laws of effectiveness.

I had to thank Bob. I ran up to him afterward and introduced myself. Come to find out, he was also a Central Washington University graduate. I shared my story and my struggles with him. He patiently listened, then looked at me and asked, "You *do* know that there is another way to live?"

That blew my mind. I felt challenged by Bob. Not only was I moved by his message, but I could see myself doing what he was doing and loving it. He showed me the vision of what I wanted to do with my life.

Immediately, I ran home to talk to Cindy. She could see my passion and excitement and said, "Honey, you love two things. You love sports, and you love speaking. Have you ever thought about speaking for a living?"

And so it began—I had found my purpose.

Little did I know that fulfilling my purpose would come with a price. Talking about the success principles was easy, but the real transformation didn't happen until I began practicing them.

You do know that there is another way to live?

The "Eat What You Kill" Sales Model

What I didn't know was that I was going to starve for the next two years. An inspired salesman, I traveled up and down the freeway persuading every company and real estate agent office to come to my seminar on how to be more successful. I cold-called, stopped by unannounced, and poured my heart out.

Although I didn't have any evidence of success to demonstrate at the time, that didn't stop me from pitching my seminar to every business I could find. Then, *finally*, it happened. My first seminar was scheduled! Seven people came, which, in comparison to the number of people I'd spoken with, was less than 1 percent.

The seminar was rough, and everything that could have gone wrong did. The start time was supposed to be 9:00 a.m., but instead everyone arrived at 8:00 a.m. and I wasn't ready. I couldn't afford to rent the audio-visual equipment at the hotel, so as people were arriving, I was carrying in my own 36-inch television and dripping in sweat. I couldn't look anyone in the eye. I quickly set it up and ran to the restroom to clean up.

As part of my value guarantee, I had offered attendees a refund if they weren't satisfied. By lunch, half of my guests asked for their money back. I didn't make enough money to even cover my expenses. This was my beginning.

To this day, I appreciate Cindy so much because she supported me through this difficult period. She would say, "My husband leaves every day to go hunting. He doesn't always come back with food, but he never comes home with bullets in his gun."

Shortly thereafter, a good friend of mine, Charlie Davis, the executive director of the local YMCA, gave me the opportunity to do a seminar with his leadership team. I was so excited! I poured everything I had into that seminar.

After the event, one of the men who'd attended went home and told his wife about it. His wife was a district manager for Starbucks and recommended me to her organization. A few days later, I had a meeting set up with Starbucks.

Can you imagine? A year earlier, I was continuously being rejected as I *begged* people to sign up for my seminar. A year later, I was the main speaker for the Starbucks store managers conference in Orlando, Florida.

I thought that achieving my dream of being a professional football player would give me fulfillment and purpose, but it paled in comparison to how I felt that day speaking to the Starbucks audience about unleashing their potential. I saw the positive impact it was having on them.

In that moment, I discovered my life's work.

> *The greatest tragedy in life is not death,*
> *but a life that never realized its full potential.*
> —Myles Munroe, *Unleashing Potential*

Dormant Ability and Unused Success

Every single one of us has potential, but it is important to understand what potential really is.

Potential is dormant ability, unused success. Everything that you can be but have not become. Everything you can do but have not done.

Potential has no retirement plan. It doesn't run out, nor is it limited by age. As you think about potential, consider all the areas of your life—as a spouse, parent, friend, and leader. What have you *not* done? What have you *not* become?

There is no such thing as an overachiever.

The great John Wooden advised that no one ever unleashes *all* their potential. He stated that your potential is unlimited, so we are all just underachievers to various degrees. In fact, there is no such thing as an overachiever, because studies show that we use less than 10 percent of our actual potential. That means 90 percent of your capability is lying dormant.

This is similar to icebergs floating in the ocean. Only 10 percent of the iceberg is visible above the water, so it is easy to overlook and ignore the remaining 90 percent that exists below the surface. We make the mistake of basing our life around the 10 percent that is visible.

Our ultimate goal is to use more. Imagine if you added just one more percent and translated it into greatness!

Potential versus Effectiveness

I love basketball. After my release from the NFL, I began playing in weekly pick-up games at the local YMCA. I remember one game in particular because I played so well. I couldn't wait to rush home and tell Cindy about it: "Baby girl, your husband was killin' it at the gym today. I mean, I was on fire! No one could stop me." I sat there for a minute and added, "Honey, I think I made a mistake. I should have worked hard to make it to the NBA. They have guaranteed contracts, they play indoors, and you can play for a long time. I would have been an incredible player. I would have been special."

As I sat there regretting not pursuing pro basketball, my wife asked a simple question: "Who did you play against today?"

"Carl, a friend of mine—but why does that matter?"

"I'm just asking a couple questions. How tall is Carl?"

"He's 5'8"—why?"

"Okay, you are 6'3". How old is Carl?"

"Honey, does this matter? He is in his forties, but he plays a lot younger."

I was in my twenties. My wife had made her point very clearly. I'd played well, but I shouldn't have used my competition as my standard of effectiveness. I should have asked myself, "How well did I play in comparison to my potential?"

> *How effective are you in comparison to your potential?*

Effectiveness is the degree to which you use your potential.

We have the tendency to measure our success as compared to other people, but we must measure our success based on our potential. In sports, you could be winning on the scoreboard and still be playing poorly—not effective compared to your potential. The question isn't how effective are you against your competition, but rather *how effective are you in comparison to your potential?*

We must strive for excellence and keep raising the bar. When you use your potential as the standard, you remove yourself from the rollercoaster of performance and allow the unleashing of more of your potential.

Natural Ability and Talent

Three ingredients make up our potential. The first ingredient is natural ability and talent. You are simply born with it. Sometimes it is hidden and must be unleashed with work and dedication, but we all have it.

There are two caveats. First, it is easier to be good and more difficult to be great. Second, we all tend to allow the "good" to get in the way of the "great."

I had the opportunity to be a keynote speaker with Malcolm Gladwell, a bestselling author and journalist, for a group of financially accomplished individuals. While Malcolm was speaking, he asked the audience, "How many of you are first-generation immigrants?" Fifty percent of the group raised their hands. He then asked, "How many of you graduated college?" Less than 30 percent raised their hands. "How many of you have ever been diagnosed with a learning disability?" Seventy percent of the group raised their hands.

This successful group of individuals had overcome significant challenges. For many of them, English wasn't even their first language. They had to be creative, take risks, and establish strong work habits.

Because your natural ability and talent don't require you to work hard, it is easier to be good at certain things. Don't be tempted to follow the path of least resistance. Be willing to put forth the necessary work and effort to become *great*.

We also have the tendency to allow the good to get in the way of being great; meaning, when we experience a taste of success, it prevents us from having even greater success because we get comfortable.

Nothing fails like success.

A dear friend calls this phenomenon "the land of good enough"—in reference to the biblical story of the Israelites. The Israelites left

Egypt to find the Promised Land, but instead they wandered for forty years in the wilderness of "the land of good enough." They kept putting off their search for the Promised Land and allowed their fear to hold them hostage from their ultimate goal.

How can you and I avoid being stuck in the "land of good enough"?

Knowledge and Education

The second ingredient of potential is knowledge and education.

We live in a day and age when knowledge is exploding—doubling every twelve months, which is mind-boggling. The caveat, though, is that knowledge is a bit overrated. If knowledge were enough from a success standpoint, then we all should be very successful, especially when all we have to do to find an answer is Google it. But it is not the knowledge that has the value—it is the *application* of that knowledge that has the value.

Ask yourself, "Do I do this?"

Knowledge can add to your success, but if you don't *apply* knowledge it does nothing for you. You will be known as an "educated derelict."

As you read the principles in this book, don't ask yourself, "Do I already know this?" Instead, ask yourself, "Do I *do* this?"

Intrinsic Motivation

The third ingredient of potential is your intrinsic, compelling urge to do or be better.

In other words, it is being motivated, to have a motive for every action. What is driving you to be more successful and to do more? Being motivated is good, but sometimes more motivation isn't what you need.

For example, the engine of a car has great potential. It propels the car to go at incredibly fast speeds, but what if every time you pushed the gas pedal down, you didn't go any faster? What's wrong?

Let's say you are motivated—pushing the gas pedal down, doing everything you are supposed to do, but your "car" isn't moving any faster. Why?

More motivation isn't the issue. *You need to release the emergency brake!*

When I played football, some games the coaches would give us the greatest motivational speech at halftime, because we had really gotten beat up in the first half. We would start the second half more motivated, but then we would just make the same mistakes faster and harder. It wasn't motivation that we needed. We needed a new strategic direction!

Sound familiar?

Unleash Potential with Responsibility

Where do you think the most valuable piece of real estate is on the planet? You might think of the South African diamond mines or the oil fields in the Middle East. Perhaps real estate in the San Francisco Bay Area comes to mind.

Actually, I believe the most valuable land on the planet is in cemeteries. Cemeteries have so much untapped potential it is overwhelming: people's ideas, dreams, inventions, cures to disease, books never written, uncovered possibilities, and resources that are now lost forever. So many people die with their potential never to be seen or shared with the world. That's sobering.

We all have potential, but the real question is… *how do you unleash it?*

The key to releasing your potential is to challenge it and give it responsibility. Potential is like muscle in the body.

We are all born with muscles, but the shape, size, and strength are dictated by how much we exercise and give muscles resistance. Muscle doesn't strengthen without resistance. When you give muscle responsibility and challenge it, it breaks down in order to build back up even stronger.

> *Resistance is the gateway to greatness.*

In the weight room of achievement, problems and obstacles are your weights.

Sometimes resistance is viewed as an indicator that you don't have what it takes, but the resistance is the gateway to greatness. It allows you to discover your potential as you confront the challenges and obstacles in your life.

If you ignore or avoid your problems, your potential will atrophy and cannot be unleashed. Those are the very things that unleash it! You must "lift" the things that you complain about.

As a leader, the same philosophy applies to your team. Don't eliminate your team's problems. Rather, get your team to look at the problems in a different way. Many times, the opportunities are simply dressed up like problems, but inside they hold the new ideas that often create the next breakthrough.

Easier ≠ Better

While speaking at an event in Manchester, England, I met a gentleman by the name of Marcus. He was in the audience and came up to me afterward because he had enjoyed hearing my message on potential. He was from Somalia and had grown up as a child warrior. The atrocities that he had seen and experienced were unimaginable.

As a teenager, he'd won a lottery to come to the United States. He started high school in Southern California and a few things immediately caught his attention. Marcus was fascinated with how many pairs of shoes his classmates owned. They would come to school wearing a different pair in the same week! He had never seen anything like that before.

His classmates also were driving cars to school, which blew his mind. He began to wonder how he could do and have similar things.

Marcus made an appointment with his school counselor and asked her a very simple, straightforward question: What could he do to experience or live a life like his classmates?

She gave him simple advice, "Get as educated as possible."

With excitement, Marcus asked, "Great! So, what is the process?"

"Graduate from high school and go to college."

"What are the best colleges around here?" he asked.

"Stanford, UCLA, Berkeley, and Pepperdine."

"I want to go there."

"Whoa, whoa, whoa…you just got here," she replied. "You are well behind the other students in language and learning." The counselor went on and on about the obstacles that Marcus would need to overcome. He sat there quietly until she said, "…and you are going to have to work really, really hard."

Marcus perked up. "Is that it? All I have to do is work really hard?"

Every day, Marcus was up at the crack of dawn. He went to school until 2:30 p.m., worked a job from 3:30 to 7:00 p.m., and finished his homework from 7:30 to 11:30 p.m. Then he got up the next morning and did it all over again. He maintained this routine for the next four years—during the summer months, too.

Marcus finished in the top level of his class, went to one of the top colleges, got a master's degree, and is now a director at one of the largest Fortune 50 companies. I was so inspired by his story!

Before our conversation ended, he said, "Eric, I have a concern. Not only do I have a concern, but my wife has this concern as well. I am worried about my kids."

"How can you be worried about your kids? Life will be so much easier for them. You have provided them with an amazing life."

"That's my concern. They won't have the same obstacles that my wife and I had, which brought the greatness out of us. Easier doesn't mean better. Easier is just easier. They won't have the same opportunities to challenge their greatness."

Marcus made an amazing point: *Easier does not equate to better.* For Marcus, overcoming those challenges brought out his potential. Those challenges gave him potential responsibility and resistance and allowed him to grow into who he is today.

Marcus's story not only emphasizes how to use challenges and obstacles to unleash our potential, but it also highlights their importance. As a leader, you don't want to remove the obstacles from your team. Instead, it is your job to get your team to see each problem as a development opportunity. Each problem needs to be solved, not removed. Removing obstacles stunts growth.

Marcus's story touched me so strongly that I even changed the way I was parenting. Kids face many obstacles, and I used to think that removing the obstacles to make things easier was the answer, but it isn't.

Easier is just easier. It is not about doing things easier; it is about doing things right.

Muscle doesn't grow with easy, light repetitions. Potential isn't released that way either. Allow challenges and problems to bring out the best in yourself, your team, and your kids. Be a leader that looks at something and doesn't see it as an obstacle, but instead sees it as an opportunity.

What development opportunities do you have in your personal and professional life right now?

Mistakes Build Resiliency

Your past mistakes can also unleash your potential. Needlessly, we worry that our mistakes invalidate our potential, but they don't. They simply add to a much greater story. Mistakes give us the opportunity to build resiliency.

Mohammed Ali once said, "So many times the champion is just the one who didn't hear the ten-second count by the referee."

All of us make mistakes. We can't avoid that, but we can learn to bounce back and keep going.

Michael Jordan, one of my favorite athletes of all time, talks about how many times he missed a shot compared to how many times he made the shot. Even with the possibility of failure, he was willing to take the last shot.

> *Mohammed Ali once said, "So many times the champion is just the one who didn't hear the ten-second count by the referee."*

I urge my daughters to never worry about mistakes. I want them to feel comfortable with being in position to make a play, take the shot, ask the question, or make a request. I want them to be willing to take the chance.

Security seekers never find it. The world is designed for risk takers. You take risks when you pursue opportunity.

Your Attitude Multiplies or Divides

As you unleash your potential, it is important to understand the influence of your attitude. You have the ability to grow and become better in any area of your life, but you must choose a can-do attitude.

Can you run a marathon? The answer is "yes." Have you done the work to prepare for it? Probably not, but you do have the ability.

Your skills and knowledge add to your greatness, but your attitude has the most impact because it either multiplies or divides the amount of potential you are utilizing.

For example, on a scale from 1–10, let's say you have a 7 for your skills, 7 for your knowledge, and 2 for your somewhat positive attitude. When we do the math, your total score is (7+7) x 2 = 28.

Using the same formula, let's change the numbers slightly. On a scale from 1–10, you have a 5 for your skills, 5 for your knowledge, and 7 for your can-do positive attitude. Now your total score is (5+5) x 7 = 70. Do you see the difference?

Now, using this formula, calculate your own real score. Is your attitude multiplying or dividing your greatness?

My wise grandmother has always told me to "quit living so far beneath your privilege." Ultimately, your attitude is a decision, and it significantly impacts the people around you. You are making the choice to either multiply your greatness or divide it.

We limit ourselves when we choose not to have a can-do attitude. Make the choice to not leave this planet with your potential still stored in you.

Visualize Your Legacy

Imagine you are holding an acorn in your hand. How does it feel? Notice the smooth body and imagine how the textured cap feels on your fingertips. When you look at it, what do you see? Do you see an acorn or does something more come to mind?

Perhaps all you see is an acorn, but what you really have in your hand is a forest of oak trees. Inside every single acorn is an oak tree, and inside that oak tree are thousands of acorns.

Now, *do you truly see what you are holding in your hand?*

Like an acorn, your potential is found within. Your potential is unlimited as long as you don't limit what you are capable of by the vision of yourself.

If you limit yourself as an oak tree instead of a forest, you are limiting the impact and influence that you could have on the people around you.

Over the years, each leader that I have worked with started as an acorn and grew into an oak tree. The intent was to bring out the best in their teams, but it first had to begin with the best in them.

Fulfill Your Promise

As we begin the first section of *Moving to Great*, we address the question of "Who am I?" and uncover the secrets of accessing your untapped potential. Simply knowing that you have potential isn't enough to unleash it. Here's why:

> An elderly man, in the final days of his life, is lying in bed alone. He awakens to see a large group of people clustered around his bed. Their faces are loving, but sad. Confused, the old man smiles weakly and whispers, "You must be my childhood friends coming to say goodbye. I'm so grateful." Moving closer, the tallest figure gently grasps the old man's hand and replies, "Yes, we are your best and oldest friends, but long ago you abandoned us. We are the unfulfilled promises of your youth. We are the unrealized hopes, dreams, and plans that you once felt deeply in your heart but never pursued. We are the unique talents that you never refined, the special gifts that you never discovered. Old friend, we have not come to comfort you, but to die with you."
>
> —*I Believe in You*

My goal is that your story will end differently than the old man's. On your death bed, I don't want your talents and gifts to die with you. Rather they can be the very thing that allows your legacy to live on.

REFLECTIONS

- Potential is hidden greatness, dormant ability, reserve power, unused success, and hidden talent.

- The three key ingredients of potential:
  - Natural ability and talent
  - Knowledge
  - Intrinsic, compelling urge to do or be better

- Potential requires responsibility and resistance to be unleashed.

- Challenges, problems, obstacles, and mistakes can unleash your potential.

Your skills and knowledge add to your effectiveness, but your attitude multiplies or divides it.

SELF-DISCOVERY QUESTIONS

1. Write down your reaction to this statement: "The easier it is to be good, the harder it is to be great." In what areas of your life do you find this to be true?

2. In what areas of your life do you have a lot of knowledge, but the application of that knowledge may be falling short?

3. What are some areas of potential in which you would like to be more effective?

4. If you weren't given any more resources, how could you better use what is already in your hand? In other words, what have you done with what you've already been given?

2

BORN TO WIN, CONDITIONED TO LOSE

How Do You Limit an Elephant?

If you were asked to keep a ten-thousand-pound elephant safe and securely in place, how would you do it? Now keep in mind, the elephant is considered one of the strongest mammals on the planet, a lumbering giant that can carry over a hundred people on its back and uproot a towering tree with its trunk. Perhaps you are considering a chain made of steel or titanium anchored in cement? What if I told you that all it would take to hold that elephant is a flimsy rope?

My youngest daughter and I went to a circus in Puyallup, Washington. An elephant was part of the show, and I was in complete awe. This animal was so large and majestic that we had to get a closer look, so we walked down to the circus floor. The elephant was tethered to a stake in the ground with a flimsy little rope around its ankle. *Huh? How is this possible?*

This made no sense, so I asked the elephant's trainer, "Help me understand how an elephant gets to this point. How can you keep it secure with this little rope?"

He explained, "When the elephant is young, we secure it with a chain attached to concrete. Because the elephant is smaller at that point, no matter how much he jerks the chain, he can't break free. We do it long enough for him to be convinced there is nothing he can do to break free. From that point on, the only thing the elephant has to feel is something around its ankle, and it won't fight against it."

Still confused, I asked, "Are we talking about the same elephant that can pull the big top up and push a car, yet when he feels a rope around his ankle, he's been *conditioned* to believe he can't break free?"

"Exactly. They don't realize they grew up."

As we continue to answer the question of "Who am I?" in this first quarter of *Moving to Great*, we now will explore how *your* conditioning and self-imposed limitations determine your level of awareness. We also will challenge the possibilities that you hold for yourself and how your attitude about this is influencing your actions and decisions.

This chapter is not about *discovering* your talent. I *know* you are talented. Here we want to ensure that your belief system and character support where your talent can take you. If you think about and list every limitation you can imagine that might be getting in the way of your achievement, how many flimsy ropes are attached to your ankle?

> *"You will never outgrow the limitations you place on yourself. They can only be raised or lowered."*
> —Bob Moawad

I believe we are all born to win. We are born to thrive, to grow, and to develop, but we are *conditioned* to lose, to settle, to sit back. Converse, the athletic shoe company, brilliantly captured this message in one of its marketing campaigns: "Champions are born, then unmade."

Unfortunately, this happens to many of us.

Has this happened to you?

The Power of Conditioning

Unfortunately for too many of us, the conditioning we received as a child was often negative and self-limiting. It was weighed down by criticism, lack of encouragment, fear, and constraint. It might have been criticizing words from a parent or destructive comments from close friends. Perhaps a teacher told you that you were incapable of something, that you "would never" do something.

Conditioning is the development of a behavioral pattern as the result of repetition of positive or negative feedback (actions or thoughts).

A young man once told me, "I'm not very artistic, I'm just not creative that way."

"How do you know you're not?" I asked.

"Well, all my life I haven't been. When I was eight years old, I was drawing and coloring a picture. My brother came over and told me how ugly it was and that I couldn't draw."

In disbelief, I blurted out, "Are you kidding me? And that is how you decided you were not artistic?"

And so it is. This one negative experience had shaped his entire, lifelong attitude about whether he could draw or not.

We can look at this story and realize how it can apply to many different areas of our lives.

Because of the conditioning process, the elephant believed that anything tied to his ankle stopped him from progressing and moving forward. The flimsy rope appeared to be a real limitation, when in fact it was a conditioned, self-imposed limitation.

In life, *real limitations* do exist. The challenge we face, however, is that we may never actually get to the real limitation because we cannot get beyond our conditioned, self-imposed limitation.

Self-imposed limitations exist only in your mind and keep you from resolving real limitations.

In the MTG process, I want you to challenge these self-imposed limitations. My mentor, Bob Moawad, once said, "You will never outgrow the limitations that you place on yourself. They can only be raised or lowered."

In this book, I will help you identify the flimsy ropes that are tied around your ankle.

Because of our conditioning, we create self-imposed limitations and allow them to live in our mind. These limitations usually don't come from your own doing but from others—even people who are no longer alive, some even who may have left this planet, but their words and the false limitations they placed on you still have the same cutting impact.

Whose limitations are living rent-free in your mind? It is important to understand that these imposed limitations are *false* and can be changed.

As children, we didn't have the ability to filter the conditioning that we experienced and only absorb the positive messages. We also misinterpreted the messages and meaning of things. It's very possible that your mom or dad didn't mean to send a negative message, but that's how you interpreted it through your childlike perspective.

- Your conditioning determines how you perceive yourself and the world.
- Self-imposed limitations are simply bad information.
- Don't allow yourself to be limited by bad information.
- The best day of your life is the day when you decide your life is your own.

Today, for everything that exists—at some point—someone said that it couldn't be done.

In the late 1800s, a father and his two sons attended a church service. In his sermon, the preacher foretold that one day men would fly with the birds. In disbelief, the father claimed this statement was heresy and walked out with his two sons, never to return.

> *The best day of your life is the day when you decide your life is your own.*

Later, in 1903, the man's two sons, Wilbur and Orville Wright, became the pioneers of aviation by achieving the first airplane flight.

What are some things that you think you can't do because of your conditioning? Are there things about yourself that you perceive as "truth" that might simply be bad information?

The Invisible Lid of Belief

Once you accept your self-limitations, they quickly become beliefs, and those beliefs are your "truth." This doesn't mean your beliefs are accurate—it just means that you are accepting them as "truth."

Your beliefs may even have been true at one time, but it doesn't mean they are still true today.

This false "reality" prevents you from moving upward, which is what I call a "lid." It is similar to the invisible ceiling that is created for fleas as part of their circus sideshow conditioning.

Normally, a flea can jump about seven inches vertically—that's more than one hundred times its height! (Imagine if we could jump that high!) To condition fleas not to jump, they are put in a tiny box. When the fleas jump, they bump against the top of the box. After a short time of this conditioning, the lid is removed and the fleas don't jump any higher. The ceiling is gone and with it the limitations, but now the fleas are conditioned to jump far below their ability.

Think of what might be limiting you right now. It could be a past failure that's convinced you, *You won't ever succeed.* Maybe it's a failed relationship that's got you believing, *You're unlovable.* Maybe it's an earlier experience that convinced you, *You'll never be a good leader.*

Chances are, that lid isn't even there any more. There's nothing holding you back except your belief.

Expand Your Awareness

In that same conversation with the elephant trainer, I asked, "As a trainer, what do you worry about?"

Jokingly, he replied, "That one day the elephant will find out that this rope couldn't hold him this whole time."

What if you found out that the flimsy rope around your ankle couldn't hold you? How would your life be different?

I was conditioned to be afraid that I never had enough, especially when it came to money. I felt like I had to hold on to every dollar. This tight grip made my fear *so real* and greatly impacted my family. I had never experienced the Great Depression, nor had I ever been homeless, but I acted like I had. This fear happened before I had experienced any limitation that validated my fear. I lived out the fear before the fear showed up!

The man named Job in the Bible experienced the same thing. He said, "What I feared has come upon me; what I dreaded has happened to me" (Job 3:25). Fear is conditioned and it is powerful! When you are consumed by fear, everything you look at screams that things will fall apart. You see all kinds of problems.

The good news is that regardless of what your life has been like up to this point, you can *choose* to condition yourself differently.

It all begins with an "I can" attitude. "Can" means that you have the ability to learn or do, but whether or not you choose to do so is up to you.

For example, can you speak five languages? You may be only fluent in one, but you have the *ability* to learn more. Having an "I can" attitude is one hundred times more important than IQ. One of the self-imposed limitations that we all have is that we tell ourselves, "I can't..."

We say what we can't do, and that puts a lid on what we can do.

> *You have the ability to learn or do, but whether or not you choose to do so, is up to you.*

Elephants can't choose to do something about their ankle rope, but you *can!* You have the ability to grow, change, and become better in any area of your life. Choose to emanate a can-do attitude. Use your "I can" attitude to release your potential and recondition yourself. Instead of being conditioned to lose, you can be conditioned to win!

High performers don't have a conditioned vision of doom and gloom. They see opportunity when confronted with difficult issues or challenges, and so can you.

Your conditioning doesn't get stronger every year. If you have been a certain way or had certain self-imposed limitations for forty years, it doesn't take forty years to condition yourself differently. Rather, it means that you have been repeating the same thoughts and habits every year, forty times.

Conditioning yourself differently is not as difficult as it seems. What happened yesterday need no longer be an excuse for what's happening today.

To improve your outcomes and begin the process of reconditioning yourself, you must first expand your awareness.

Awareness is defined as how clearly you perceive and understand everything that affects your life. It is a result of a lifetime of conditioning, includes your genetic makeup, and is continually changing as you experience new things.

Your current awareness is the sum total of your lifetime experiences and background. Some components affecting your awareness are genetic makeup, cultural biases, prejudices, lifetime conditioning, and family traditions. Your awareness informs your belief and value system as well as your actions and decisions. As a result, your actions and decisions (behaviors) are only as wise as the information they are based on (awareness).

What if some of the information that has informed your current awareness is inaccurate or misleading?

Bad information creates bad decisions.

What if some of the information that has informed your current awareness is inaccurate or misleading? Give yourself the chance to expand your awareness and gain greater clarity about yourself, others, and the world around you. Be willing to reevaluate your current beliefs and self-imposed limitations.

The truth is that some of the information you have is inaccurate and incomplete, and this bad information is creating poor outcomes. When you improve the information that is feeding your awareness, you immediately improve your actions and decisions.

In Appendix A, I have included an exercise that will assist you in expanding your awareness. This exercise allows you to take a personal awareness inventory of yourself as you are right now in your life. Check it out!

Your awareness must grow and to do that, you must expose yourself to new information.

Expose Yourself to New Possibilities

While consulting at Hickam Air Force Base in Hawaii, I met a colonel from South Central Los Angeles. I asked him, "When did you know that you wanted to go into the military?"

"It wasn't really the military," the officer responded. "It just happened to be the path I took. When I was in tenth grade, I went on a field trip that influenced me."

"What do you mean?"

"My whole life, I had grown up in South Central Los Angeles, so to me that was going to be my entire world. I didn't know there was more possibility. I had not been exposed to anything new."

"What changed for you?" I prodded.

"When I went on this field trip with my school to Fresno, California…"

"Fresno?" That didn't seem too eye-expanding to me.

"I know, it doesn't sound like much, but it was the greatest trip I had ever taken in my life. Especially for someone who had never been out of the city before, out of his neighborhood. I had never seen hills like that. I'd never seen windmills. I had never seen possibilities. The trip triggered something in me to where I asked myself, 'How could I see more?' That is when the military became a legitimate option. I got exposure that the world was bigger than South Central Los Angeles."

This colonel was *exposed* to new information and allowed his awareness to grow and shift. He expanded the possibilities for himself by challenging his conditioning. He opened himself up to new information and a different perspective. If he hadn't been exposed to this new environment with new people and different ideas, he would have simply created a life for himself based on his current exposure, what he had always been accustomed to.

Is there somewhere you need to visit, a person you need to meet, or new information you need to open yourself to? How can you expose yourself to something new?

I Am Stuck Here

While I was playing in the NFL, several friends and I were asked to speak in what's known as the "concrete jungle" in South Central Los Angeles. I remember going through Nickerson Gardens, Jordan Downs, and Imperial Courts—beautiful names, but very difficult places.

We spoke to kids at various schools, and I remember a young man who was standing next to me after one of our seminars. He opened up to me about his experience and his difficult circumstances. He talked about the crime and how many people die.

As we continued giving seminars throughout the day, I asked each class how many of them knew someone who had passed away. In every class, every hand went up. It was heartbreaking.

Toward the end of the day, I had the opportunity to speak to one of the eleventh graders. "What do you want to do with your life?" I asked him.

"I don't know. I am stuck here."

"What do you mean stuck?"

"Man, there is no getting out of this prison. I am stuck."

I pointed outside a window. "But there is a bus stop right there, and there is a recruiting office for the military right over there."

He wasn't interested. He had created a self-imposed, imaginary limitation that convinced him there was a wall a thousand feet high, cutting off his neighborhood from the rest of the world. He had sentenced himself to die there.

How are the stories of the colonel from South Central Los Angeles and the high school student similar? Different?

To improve an action or decision, you must first expand your awareness. Expose yourself to new experiences and information, because you might not have the whole story about yourself and the world around you.

Always be willing to challenge the information that is informing your awareness and be ready to expand the possibilities for yourself.

Get Out of Your Chicken Coop

A farmer caught a young eagle and brought it home to live with his chickens on the farm. Being surrounded by chickens, the eagle began to act like a chicken, even though its wingspan measured well over fifteen feet.

Five years passed and a naturalist came to visit the farmer. As they passed the chicken coop, the naturalist saw the eagle and said, "That bird is an eagle, not a chicken!"

"I know," said the farmer. "But it believes it is a chicken."

"But it is still an eagle," the naturalist interjected. "It has the heart of an eagle, and it is meant to soar high up in the sky."

Unimpressed, the farmer responded, "Like I said, it believes it is a chicken. It will never fly."

After much discussion, they agreed to challenge the eagle's conditioning. The naturalist picked up the eagle, and with great intensity commanded, "Eagle, you belong to the sky. Stretch forth your wings and fly!" The eagle looked to the left, looked to the right, and then jumped down to join the chickens feeding. Discouraged, the naturalist vowed to try it again the following day.

The next morning, the naturalist took the eagle to the top of the house, and again, with great intensity commanded, "Eagle, you belong to the sky. Stretch forth your wings and fly!" Unmotivated, the eagle dropped down to join the chickens in the chicken coop.

"I told you so!" the farmer bragged.

"Give me one more chance," pleaded the naturalist. "It will fly tomorrow."

The naturalist woke up early that next morning and took the eagle away from the farm to a beautiful mountainside. He picked up the eagle and again commanded, "Eagle, you belong to the sky. Stretch forth your wings and fly!" The eagle looked around as if it remembered something, but it still didn't fly. Determined, the naturalist pointed the eagle to the rising sun. Suddenly, the eagle stretched forth its wings and took off, letting out a screech as it climbed higher and higher into the endless sky.

Sometimes we need help to be exposed to new opportunities. Like this eagle, we have been conditioned to think and live at a much lower level than what we're capable of. Is there someone in your life who has convinced you that you are a chicken? Do you fly above the chicken coops in your life? Don't be content with the life of a chicken. Be willing to stretch forth your wings and fly!

I promise—you will find nothing in this book that will teach you to live among the chickens! *Moving to Great* is all about helping you recognize your eagle wings in order to fly *above* the chicken coops of life. As an eagle, you might choose to revisit the chicken coop for a meal, but you'll never again spend the night!

REFLECTIONS

- We are all born to win. We are born to thrive, to grow, and to develop. But we are conditioned to lose, to settle, and to sit back.

- Conditioning is the development of a behavioral pattern that is the result of repetition of positive or negative feedback (actions or thoughts).

- Negative and self-limiting conditioning creates "blind spots," which are a sensory blocking out of your environment based on conditioning or preconceived expectations.

- Self-limitations become beliefs, but this doesn't mean your beliefs are accurate.

- The process of conditioning yourself differently begins with awareness.

- Bad information creates bad actions and decisions.

- Expose yourself to new information and expand the possibilities for yourself.

SELF-DISCOVERY QUESTIONS

In order to exercise better control of your life, you must know *who* you really are and *what* you really want. It is necessary to ask yourself questions that you normally wouldn't ask.

Growing up, my father taught me not to confuse experience with wisdom. He advised that many people don't grow from their experiences, but rather they become bitter and resentful. My father counseled that wisdom is a result of *reflection* upon your experience.

These questions, as well as the additional questions in the appendices at the back of the book, will give you the opportunity to reflect and invest some wisdom into your future to improve your life.

1. Who are you? List 10–12 descriptive qualities about yourself.
2. Which of the qualities you listed do you like most?

3. What attitude, habits, or traits would you want to change about yourself?

4. Who is the one person (living or dead) that you like the most and why? What is it about her or him that you admire?

5. Who is the happiest person you know? How does this person influence you?

6. When were you the happiest to be alive? What were you doing and where? Who were you with?

3

CHANGE IS CONSTANT

Unpredictable and Inevitable

Change isn't new, but the speed of it is. In this new reality, not only is change getting quicker, but it is also coming at a cost. Everything is spinning at such a pace, it is easy to get distracted and lose sight of where you are intending to go. You must learn to *adapt*.

When I say adapt, I don't mean that you "go along to get along." I mean that regardless of whether the change is personal or professional, *you* make that change successful.

Change is to shift, transform, convert, substitute, exchange, or evolve. It involves various aspects of all of these words.

Every one of us is going through all kinds of change. This can include personal change as well as professional change. Some of these descriptions for organizational and personal change include:

- Marriage
- Divorce
- New relationship or the ending of an old one
- Health of yourself or a family member
- Children moving out of the home
- Children moving back in the home
- Birth of a child
- A new job
- The loss of a job

- Culture change
- Customer focus
- Globalization
- Teaming
- Workforce diversity
- Reengineering
- LEAN
- Acquisition
- Merger

Continuous change is the only constant in most of our lives and organizations, and it is taking place at a rate never before seen in history. Navigating personal and professional change is a prerequisite for success.

Take a moment to identify some of the changes currently affecting your personal and professional life. How have these changes impacted you and the people around you?

> *In times of change, learners inherit the earth while the learned, those who are know-it-alls, are beautifully equipped to deal with a world that no longer exists.*
> —Eric Hoffer

Change happens with or without you. As one thing changes, many other things change at the same time. Because change causes the past to be different from the present and the future to be different from the present, an element of uncertainty or fear creeps into your mind, because change takes you out of your comfort zone.

If you are not changing for the better, you are changing for the worse.

During changing times, we can depend on one thing: unpredictability. If you are not changing for the better, you are changing for the worse. When you are no longer a victim of change, not only can you prepare for it, but you can also take advantage of it.

Remember, you were born to win, but conditioned to lose. *Outside of the fear of loud noises and the fear of falling, you weren't born with fear.* All your other fears have been learned. This conditioned fear hinders your ability to unleash more of your potential and leverage the change in your life.

With the MTG process, you will realize that change is your ally. You will now have the tools to transform your mind to make better decisions, choose improved actions, and experience better outcomes.

Two Ways to Learn and Grow

When you think about changes that have taken place in your life, how did they affect you? Did you resist the change or accept it? Did it change your life for the better or worse?

It's certainly true that sometimes learning and growth can have a cost associated with them, but the value that we get in return is priceless. When it comes to growth and learning, there are two categories of events that encourage people to change. These moments and events can unleash the potential that is lying dormant within all of us. One category is Significant Learning Moments (SLM) and the second is Significant Life Events (SLE).

Significant Learning Moments are moments that carry the potential of creating positive change in your life.

These moments are the *best way to learn,* because the price you pay for these lessons is simply your *attention,* and the rewards are infinite. It has been said that if we study such moments and pay more attention, we will realize that these moments deliver a tremendous amount of insight.

Reading this book and studying the MTG principles is an example of a Significant Learning Moment. The cost of learning is low. Other examples that can allow for positive change in your life include:

- Good books
- Movies
- Life stories
- Conversations
- The experiences of others (this is a big one!)

In my life, there are three Significant Learning Moments that stick out in my mind. My first SLM was being the father of two beautiful daughters, Taylor and Madison.

I had the opportunity to learn about parenting from one of my mentors, Richard Anderson. Richard and his wife, Patty, have three daughters that have grown into tremendous women. They are amazing wives and mothers and successful in everything they do. I have always been amazed with how comfortable they are in their skin, and I always wanted my daughters to exude that confidence and ease.

Richard shared one piece of advice with me in regards to parenting: "Eric—keep this in mind: Self-esteem first, self-discipline second."

I'll never forget that because it taught me the importance of self-esteem and how it acts as the foundation to then create discipline in all aspects of life. That one piece of advice has allowed my wife and me to parent in a way that strengthens our daughters' self-esteem and builds their self-confidence.

My second SLM was related to my health. I will never forget meeting a gentleman by the name of Charlie Blake at my local gym. At the time, he was in his fifties and in tremendous shape. I was in my early thirties and wanted to know his secret to staying in such great condition. "What's your secret?" I asked.

"The key to staying in shape is to *never* get out of shape," he confidently replied.

I took his advice to heart and haven't been out of shape yet. This Significant Learning Moment had very little cost, but has produced huge benefits.

My third SLM concerned my financial life. It was a simple book that cost me less than three dollars. The title is *The Richest Man in Babylon*, and it took me only an hour and a half to read. Only ninety minutes of time for a priceless impact on my family's financial life!

Has something like that ever happened to you?

Significant Life Events are learning events that create an unexpected and unplanned change in your life.

These events are a crisis of some kind and typically come with a high price. You are forced to pay a large sum for "learning tuition" as you adjust to the outcome of the change. Some examples would be you or a family member being diagnosed with a health condition, you losing your job, or your spouse asking for a divorce.

Remember, the tuition cost of a SLE is high, but the tuition cost of a SLM is much lower. Your payment is simply your attention. We too often ignore the Significant Learning Moments that life presents to us until it is too late, and then we are faced with a Significant Life Event.

For example, perhaps your spouse is consistently asking to spend more time with you. Do you choose to ignore it or pay attention? If you pay attention, the *return* is high. If you ignore it, the *cost* is high. Ignored SLMs can become painful SLEs.

SLMs allow for infinite growth at a bargain of a price. These moments have the ability provide you with a learning experience as well as unleash your potential.

Study your moments. Pay attention to the details. To start, use this book and experience it as a Significant Learning Moment. Take the time to reflect and study moments in your life that hold informational value that you haven't discovered yet.

What have been some Significant Learning Moments and/or Significant Life Events when you changed your attitudes, habits, or behaviors? What have been some when you haven't?

> *Take time to gather up your past so that you can draw*
> *from your experiences and invest them in your future."*
> —Jim Rohn

Why Do We Resist Change?

There are five predominant reasons why potential is not unleashed and why people don't change. These reasons get in the way of transformation and growth. As you explore the MTG principles, not only will you learn how to embrace change, but you also will learn how to create long-lasting change within yourself. You will learn how to change from the inside out.

Review these reasons why we resist change and see if you recognize any of these attitudes within yourself.

1. I'm okay the way I am.
2. I fear the unknown.
3. I fear failure.
4. I fear rejection.
5. I don't know how to change.

I'm Okay the Way I Am

Change is difficult. Some people are unwilling to change while others are willing but lack the tools and confidence. It is important to consider the possibility that maybe it isn't the change that is causing the resistance. The "I'm okay the way I am" attitude creates resistance and a lack of drive and desire for greatness. It is a sense of contentment and comfort.

This attitude is conditioned and makes people feel limited. They start to believe that this is as good as it gets, so they work hard to protect what currently exists. Unfortunately, it is a thief of greatness.

*Your current success **can** get in the way of your reaching greater success. It can prevent your acorn from manifesting into a forest of oak trees.*

This passive attitude could be parallel to "coasting." Coasting is okay at times, but it usually means you are going downhill.

When someone says, "I'm okay just the way I am," it's another way of saying, "I am not the one who needs to improve, adapt, or adjust. I am a great leader—it's these idiots I have to lead who need to change. I am a great husband—it's my wife who needs to realize how good she has it. Our products and services are fine—it's our customers who have the problem."

Coasting is okay at times, but it usually means you are going downhill.

The late, great philosopher Eric Hoffer reminded us that in times of change, it is the learners who move forward victorious while the coasters find themselves drifting downhill to a world that no longer exists.

Leaders are learners, and learners are earners. If you're willing to learn, you'll continually increase your earnings because you'll be finding new ways to add value. This is also true for organizations. A learning organization is a growing organization; a growing organization is an earning organization. Conversely, the second you believe that you know it all and have no need to expand your knowledge and skills, you are embracing a very limited and dangerous mindset.

In football there is a defensive formation called the prevent defense. The prevent defense is what teams use once they get a lead, and their goal is to hold onto that lead and run out the clock while the other team has the ball. This defense allows short gain plays in an effort to prevent long gain plays.

When you operate from a prevent defense mindset, instead of preventing yourself from losing, you are actually preventing yourself from winning, because the scoreboard is always a lagging indicator. The scoreboard is a reflection of what you have already done and not a reflection of what you are currently doing. This approach kills your momentum, and it is just a matter of time before it shows up on the scoreboard.

During my playing days, in games when we were holding on in order to win, we could feel the momentum shift even though the scoreboard was still in our favor. In those moments, all we could hope for was that the clock would run out.

The "I'm okay the way I am" attitude prevents you from truly maximizing your greatness and embracing change.

As part of our new reality today of constant change, the greatest challenge that you face is the changing expectations of customers or clients, regardless of your business or product line. Customer expectations are changing every day, and those expectations aren't always influenced by you. Since when has your next door neighbor's Google review about a company potentially had more influence and impact than a $50 million marketing budget? We have never seen a time where one customer had this much influence.

As the customer's influence has increased, so have expectations. Last year, what was considered *exceeding* the customer's expectation is now only *meeting* their expectation, which in effect is the new definition of mediocrity. Because of this phenomenon, your goal should be continuous improvement. If you don't do this, you will be left behind.

What you accomplished last year isn't good enough this year. If meeting expectations becomes your normal, you are in danger of becoming a commodity just like everything else.

As long as you live, keep learning how to live.
—Seneca

I Fear the Unknown

You may not have realized this, but fear and selfishness go hand in hand. By this I mean that, like most humans, you are more concerned with how something will affect you than how it will benefit the greater good. Life is about self-preservation.

*When you fear the unknown, you tend to **choose** unhappiness over uncertainty.*

We would rather be unhappy and safe rather than take the risk of going through a period of uncertainty to go after what we really want. We say to ourselves, "I might be unhappy, but at least I am certain about it."

This fear-based mindset causes paralysis of the brain and heart. We complain about our problems and challenges and do nothing about them. When the future looks uncertain, we cling even harder to what currently exists. We fight and resist change in order to maintain the status quo, even though it is far beneath our capability. We stay in an unhealthy relationship and trap ourselves in a career we can't stand.

When my father passed away, I had a strong fear of uncertainty. I didn't know what the future was going to look like without my dad. My mother struggled as well. We had to navigate through those feelings until we were strong enough to choose the new reality.

As a leader, when you push for change but have not given the people around you a solid picture of what the future looks like, you will wonder why you are encountering resistance. People resist change because the promise of the change is unfulfilled. With every lackluster change effort in the workplace, employees become skeptical that what is being promised will actually occur. So when a change effort fails, you might be tempted to place the blame on them, but the fault is most likely your own.

It is critical that you provide a clear picture of what the future will look like and eliminate uncertainty. Visualize the future and design it in your mind. Then share it creatively. You must create vision both for yourself and your team.

I Fear Failure

I joke that "if at first you don't succeed, set blame quick!" I'm not serious, but this is often our mindset because there is so much pressure to get it all right the first time. Or the fear of failure will often prevent you from acting in the first place, and it will get in the way of releasing your potential.

Because of your fear of failure, perhaps you are avoiding a tough conversation with someone you love or a coworker. Maybe your fear is stopping you from asking for a promotion or applying for a more challenging position. Perhaps you have thought about changing your career or learning how to play golf. The cost of such inaction is expensive!

Take a moment to reflect on your life:

What has the fear of failure cost you?

What are the things that you could have or should have but don't have because of fear?

What could you be doing or should be doing but are not doing because of fear?

Fear of failure is expensive.

Fear of failure is actually a self-image issue, because your self-image reveals what you believe to be true about yourself. If you don't believe you are capable of or deserve your goal, the fear of failure holds you hostage. You do nothing and pay the cost of fear.

If you believe you are capable and do deserve your goal, even when you make a mistake or things don't work out, you will dust yourself off and try again. Do you see the difference?

Because failure is simply part of life, we must redefine it and replace our fear with resiliency.

Accomplishing a goal requires a certain level of resiliency in order to overcome the many risks, obstacles, and setbacks along the way. And nothing so significantly hinders our ability to be resilient than fear.

For me, public failure has always been one of my greatest fears. When I look back on my NFL career, part of me feels like a failure. After two years with the New York Jets, a failed stint with the San Diego Chargers, and one year with the Green Bay Packers, I was fired and "promoted" to fan.

I have also had public disappointment where I dropped a pass in front of 80,000 fans who were expecting me to make the play. After the ball went straight through my hands, the crowd didn't hesitate to express their frustration by booing and yelling at me.

I chuckle when I am asked if I get nervous speaking in front of large audiences. It is a fair question, because I have spoken in front of twenty to thirty thousand people. But my answer is "absolutely not." After being booed by 80,000 fans in New York City, there is nothing that an audience could do to phase me.

I Fear Rejection

The fear of rejection prevents change, because it obstructs the exchange of sufficient, accurate, and candid feedback. Although you might fear rejection and the opinion of others, you must learn to minimize it.

Interestingly, a lack of proper self-esteem works with the fear of rejection to foster resistance to change, so building high self-esteem is a priority.

Your self-esteem is your psychological immune system, so when it's not at the level it should be, you will have the tendency to raise the opinions of others above your own, as well as create your own opinion from the opinions of others.

Instead of viewing feedback as a negative experience that you need to shield yourself from, welcome it and realize it is a very positive thing.

When your self-esteem is low, it hinders your ability to give feedback as well as receive it. When you receive feedback, you are preoccupied with the need to protect yourself with defensiveness. When you give feedback, you don't have the confidence to be honest and constructive.

Instead of viewing feedback as a negative experience that you need to shield yourself from, welcome it and realize it is a very positive thing. It provides you with the opportunity to bridge the gap between your current self and your potential.

Relationships often remain damaged because people aren't willing to have conversations and exchange feedback. They function without feedback and assume things are okay rather than asking and gaining insight. We either shrink or reject people before they can reject us.

As we continue to explore fear and its impact during the MTG process, it is important to understand that unknowns, failure, and rejection go hand in hand with success. The two biggest destroyers of success are the fear of failure and the fear of rejection. The fear of failure destroys your self-image, and the fear of rejection destroys your self-esteem.

*You must realize that in order to reach your end goal, you have to experience some uncertainty, failure, and rejection. They aren't things you can avoid on your journey, but you can overcome the *fear* of them.*

Sometimes I am fearful about having crucial conversations with my daughters, but I love my daughters. Because my love for them is infinitely stronger than my fear of being rejected by them, I am able to move past my fear and have those tough and sometimes uncomfortable conversations.

Love is a stronger emotion than fear.

We cannot escape fear. We can only transform it into a companion that accompanies us on our exciting adventures...Take a risk today—one small or bold stroke that will make you feel great once you have done it.
—Susan Jeffers

I Don't Know How to Change

Sometimes you just don't know how to change. Perhaps you have the willingness, but you lack the skills and knowledge. This is the very reason for *Moving to Great*, which provides tools of transformation that enable you to thrive in times of change, as well as make desired changes in your personal and professional life.

MTG is a logical sequential process that is in alignment with the laws of effectiveness. There are laws that govern our physical world like gravity, mass and momentum, and cause and effect—to name a few, but there are also laws that govern human effectiveness, and we act upon them according to our level of awareness.

How much do you know about the laws of human effectiveness?

Level One: "I Don't Know, and I Don't Know I Don't Know."

The laws of human effectiveness govern the outcome of your decisions and actions, whether or not you are aware of them or not. It is only when you become aware of something that you can recognize a need.

At level one, you are ignorant and unaware. This is the lowest level of competency. The challenge is that you are still responsible for your actions and decisions.

When I first got married, I was unconsciously incompetent. I didn't know what I didn't know. Not only did I not know, but I didn't know that I didn't know. Not only is it very difficult to build a solid relationship from this level of ignorance, but it is also a bad idea to *argue* from this level of ignorance.

Level Two: "I Don't Know, and I Know I Don't Know."

Due to the clear and consistent performance feedback from my wife, Cindy (smile), it didn't take me long to graduate to the second level of competency in my marriage. At this level, you are at least aware of your ignorance, which is a plus. When you don't know, but you know you don't know, you can begin to learn and change.

Conscious incompetency creates a fever and an awareness that points to a need that wants to be met. It causes us to pursue, reach out, and learn because we realize that there is a gap. It creates an internal sense of urgency.

This is a good level. You know there is a need to improve, and you are willing to address it. Like Eric Hoffer advised, it's the learners who inherit the earth.

Level Three: "Things Are Working, But I Don't Know Why."

At the third level of competency, you make appropriate decisions and act accordingly, but the challenge is that you aren't sure why things are working. This of course makes it difficult to repeat your success, teach it, or share it.

I actually find this to be a very interesting level. I encounter many dynamic and effective leaders from all over the world who are really good at what they do and have a positive influence on those around them, but when I ask them how they do it, they can't give me an explanation. So, if performance begins to slide, it is very hard for them to get back on track because they don't know why things were working beforehand.

We are always willing to examine our setbacks, but we need to demonstrate the same intensity when examining our successes. I like to call this a "success autopsy," because you need to metaphorically slice it open to examine its parts in order to better understand what is happening on the inside.

I am amazed at how much time and money organizations, leaders, coaches, and individuals spend on areas of weakness, and how little time they spend on evaluating areas of strength. In order to be successful, you must study and inspect your areas of strength. Gain an understanding of what you are doing right and how it can be replicated, so that you can teach it to others.

There was a time early in my marriage when my wife, Cindy, was happier than usual. I could tell that she was floating on cloud nine. It was amazing except there was a problem. I had absolutely no idea why she was so happy! It made me really nervous. I wanted to ask her about it, but I didn't want to disrupt it either.

Eventually, I decided to ask her because I needed to know what I was doing right. It was a conversation that I will never forget. She gave me great insight into what I was doing right and allowed me to become consciously competent, which is the next level.

I urge you to shine a light on and study your successes. When things are working, you need to *know* why.

When things are working, you need to know why.

Level Four: "I Know, and I Know that I Know."

At competency level four, you have developed skills and identified the appropriate behaviors and actions for success. You now know why your choices, behaviors, and actions get certain results. Unfortunately, it isn't enough to just know.

Knowing is only half of the equation.

Do you know more about good communication than you demonstrate in your interactions with others? Do you know more about nutrition and exercise than is evidenced by your daily habits?

In my previous example, I was able to discover the why behind my wife's pleasant mood, but I still had the challenge of consistently using that knowledge to affect my actions. The key word here is consistent. Just because I now know what to do, it doesn't necessarily mean that I am always going to do it.

This is called the knowing–doing gap. Do not confuse knowing something with actually doing something.

As you continue to study the MTG principles, you may say to yourself, "I know this." But my question for you is, "But, do you *do* this?" Too often we stop at knowing, and knowing doesn't create results.

Level Five: "I Know, and I Know That I Know, and I Have Turned It Over to Being Natural, Free-flowing, Spontaneous, and Consistent!"

This level is your ultimate goal. You know what it takes to be a good leader and communicator, you've been consistently doing it, and now it has become a habit. You don't have to think about it anymore, you just do it. It is natural, free-flowing, spontaneous, and consistent. It has become a part of your identity. You aren't *trying* to be a good leader or communicator; you *are* a good leader and communicator. Can you imagine this?

You get to level five by training and daily practice. My goal is to go from knowing what it takes to be a good husband to actually being a good husband. I already know what it takes to have a great marriage, but knowing isn't enough. I need to incorporate daily habits. Instead of *trying* to be a good husband, I am going to *train* to be a good husband.

Remember, the MTG process is your training camp, and this book is your playbook. Ingrain this into the way you think. This level is about creating a way of life and a certain way of thinking, so that you then consistently can behave this way.

If you find yourself stuck at level four, don't be too hard on yourself. This takes practice.

MTG is a journey of transformation in how you *think, act,* and *feel.* It is a process of changing from the inside out and improving your outcomes.

As a leader, it is important to understand that organizations don't change; *people* in the organization change.

> Let it be noted that there is no more delicate matter to take in hand, nor more dangerous to conduct, nor more doubtful in its success, than to set up as a leader in the introduction of changes. For he who innovates will have for his enemies all those who are well off under the existing order of things, and only lukewarm supporters in those who might be better off under the new."
> —Niccolò Machiavelli, *The Prince*

REFLECTIONS

- Change is inevitable.

- Significant Learning Moments only require your attention and prevent a high-priced Significant Life Event.

- Barriers to change:
  - I'm okay the way I am.
  - I fear the unknown.
  - I fear failure.
  - I fear rejection.
  - I don't know how to change.

- Coasting requires you to be going downhill.

- The new definition of mediocrity is "meeting expectations."

- People tend to choose unhappiness over uncertainty.

- Redefine failure and replace your fear with resiliency.

- Uncertainty, failure, and rejection go hand in hand with success. You can't avoid them, but you can avoid fearing them.

SELF-DISCOVERY QUESTIONS

1. What are some of the changes going on now in your life?

2. What has been the effect of these changes on the people around you? (Examples: fear, excitement, stress, confusion, etc.)

3. How can you remove or overcome the barriers to change?

4. Have you created room for mistakes on your journey?

5. Have you explained to the people around you why change is happening and what the benefits are?

6. Have you made the unknown known? Have you given as much clarity as possible to what the future could look like?

7. Do you facilitate a culture of teamwork and collaboration?

8. Do you allow for feedback?

9. Do you support the change and growth of people around you?

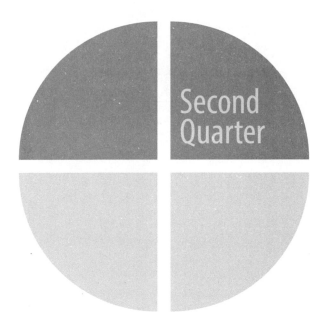

Second
Quarter

How Did I Get Here?

4

THE MAGNIFICENT MIND

Thinking Is Your Best Asset

Let's begin the second quarter of *Moving to Great*. We started with addressing the question, "Who am I?" Now in Chapter Four, we explore, "How did I get here?" You will learn about how your mind works and the impact of your attitude, self-image, and self-esteem.

Your willpower always fights a losing battle against your belief system, so you must learn new skills to make lasting positive changes. It is time to program your most important tool and asset: your mind.

How do you unleash your incredible potential? *It begins with the way you think.*

At the University of Chicago, Dr. Benjamin Bloom studied the top twenty-five sculptors, Olympic swimmers, concert pianists, research neurologists, mathematicians, and tennis players under thirty-five years of age. He expected to uncover incredible natural talents and ability, but his study actually revealed that determination, persistence, passion, and nurturing were far more important than talent in achieving success. It wasn't their talent that made them the best in the world; it had more to do with the way they *thought*.

> *"So far as a man thinks, he is free."*
> —Ralph Waldo Emerson

Many great philosophers and successful people have come to the same realization. Dr. Walter Staples confirms that the quality of thinking that guides your intelligence is far more important than the amount of intelligence you actually have.

The Bible counsels, "As a man thinketh in his heart, so is he." (Proverbs 23:7)

Sigmund Freud established that thought is action in rehearsal.

Henry Ford said it best: "Thinking is hard work. That is why so few people do it."

The way you think defines your level of success, because even when you give yourself a new start or move to a different location, your way of thought follows. You can change your external circumstances, but the challenge is that you take *you* with you wherever you go.

How Your Mind Works

Many people do not consider how they think or the parts of the thought process, but it is important to understand in order to influence our thinking.

To create change, we attempt to inspire our willpower, but it doesn't work.

Every January we come up with New Year's resolutions that we don't follow through on. Can you relate? We believe that when we consciously decide on something, it means something has been done. We have discovered that is not necessarily true.

Your mind has three distinct parts that make up the thought process:

1. Conscious

Your conscious mind associates and evaluates data and stimuli. It stores only information that it determines to be of value. It perceives, evaluates, associates, and then decides. It is a great process. When you make a decision, you evaluate it and associate what you have experienced in the past and then you make a decision. The challenge is that your conscious mind is only responsible for a tiny percent of your perception and behavior. We think we are being objective in our decision-making, but we really aren't.

2. Subconscious

Your subconscious mind stores your "reality" and handles all of your automatic habits and behaviors. It is like a large storage data container that is nonjudgmental, meaning it doesn't complete an analytic decision-making process and form a conclusion. It simply holds the data. It doesn't filter, sort, assess, or evaluate it. It is responsible for the vast majority of your perception and behavior.

3. Creative Subconscious

Your creative subconscious mind exists to resolve conflict, reduce tension, and to creatively solve problems. Its goal is to make sure you act like you. It provides the drive and energy to maintain your "reality," whether or not that reality is in your best interest. In other words, your creative subconscious ensures that the attitudes and stored beliefs of your inner world match the perceptions of your outer world. When it doesn't match, your creative subconscious eliminates the inconsistency with problem-solving and conflict resolution.

As a practical example, pretend there is someone that you think doesn't like you. You see this person through the filter of this premise. All of their actions and behaviors are perceived in relationship to your belief that they don't like you.

What happens when this person does something nice to you? Do you challenge your belief? No, typically what we do is think they are up to something. Something smells fishy.

People are more rationalizing than rational.

We gather information to prove that our beliefs are true.

Goal Attainment

Every single one of us is a goal-setter by nature, whether we do it intentionally or unintentionally.

Goal-setting is a conscious act, whereas goal attainment is a subconscious act.

When you set a goal, your conscious mind is engaged, but the parts of your mind that allow you to *attain* the goal are the subconscious and creative subconscious minds. Your creative subconscious mind allows you to reckon, see, and draw into your life the circumstances, scenarios, situations, and resources that are consistent with your most dominant beliefs. That is why your dominant belief system matters so much.

Goal attainment is similar to the Global Positioning System (GPS) system. When you use GPS, as soon as you enter the coordinates of your destination, it immediately goes to work to find you a route. Similarly, once the mind gives a goal to the subconscious mind, that goal becomes a priority to the creative subconscious mind.

If you don't give your subconscious mind a goal, your creative subconscious mind will work hard to maintain what currently exists. This is why you must change from the inside out. If you don't change the dominant beliefs in your subconscious mind, you have no other recourse but to keep experiencing a "rerun episode." Over and over… and over again.

One of my favorite TV shows from the seventies was a sitcom called *What's Happening!!* My favorite character's name was Rerun, because he kept repeating twelfth grade over and over. This is often what happens to us—we repeat the same experience year after year! Until you give your mind new things to work on, it works hard to maintain what is currently taking place.

Your mind works extremely hard to determine what to pay attention to and when not to pay attention. Your conscious mind can only focus on a limited number of stimuli at a given time, so your subconscious mind helps with the filtering process. It filters the information and decides what has value and what does not while acting in alignment with your dominant thoughts.

Conscious versus Subconscious

Your conscious mind has a limited processing capacity with a short-term memory of about twenty seconds. At most, your conscious mind can manage between one to three events at a time, and your thought impulses travel between 120 to 140 miles per hour (mph) on average. The conscious mind can process 2,000 bits of information per second.

All of this might sound impressive, but in comparison to your subconscious mind, the conscious mind is quite limited. The conscious mind is great at planning, but terrible at getting anything done. We see this all the time in organizations. Leadership teams are great at making plans, and they think that because they have a plan something will actually happen. But most of the time nothing much happens.

Your subconscious mind has an expanded processing capacity. It holds your long-term memory, which includes your experiences, attitudes, values, and beliefs. It manages thousands of events at one time and has the ability to process over 4 million bits of information per second. Your thought impulses travel at over 100,000 mph.

In organizations, the subconscious mind is expressed as the culture. Peter Drucker said, "Culture eats strategy for breakfast." Regardless of what plans have been made, the culture will determine the success. This is why creating change with the conscious mind alone doesn't work.

Belief systems in the subconscious mind have a much greater influence on behavior than willpower in the conscious mind.

As you can see, the subconscious mind is extremely powerful and completely dominates the capacity of the conscious mind. When it comes to change, it is apparent why the conscious mind only accounts for a tiny amount, and the subconscious mind accounts for the vast majority. This is why willpower comes in second to your belief system. Willpower relies on the conscious mind, whereas your belief system relies on the subconscious mind.

The key to change is learning how to train your subconscious mind (belief system) to work for you instead of against you. You must learn to use its incredible capacity for problem solving, goal attainment, and creativity to assist you in reaching your goals faster versus maintaining the status quo.

Everything we do from this point on in the MTG process is focused on using your subconscious mind (belief system) to make change happen faster.

> *We operate in the world mostly on autopilot, doing the same things today…that didn't work yesterday. When you get the correct operating thoughts into the subconscious, you will become what you are capable of becoming.*
>
> —Bob Moawad

Lock On, Lock Out

You have the capability to use your built-in filter system in your subconscious mind to lock on or lock out information that is not relevant or a priority for you. This creates what we call a "blind spot."

Imagine a mother with her child at a busy playground. There are over fifty children playing, yet through all of the noise, she immediately hears her child start to cry. She's using her mind's built-in filter to screen out the noise and key in on her child crying.

You lock on to the information that you consider valuable, and you lock out information you do not perceive as valuable.

Similar responses happen to all of us. When you buy a new car, during the first few days afterwards, it feels like you are the only one driving it. But all of a sudden, you see that same vehicle all over the road! Pregnant women experience the same phenomenon: As soon as they are pregnant, they notice pregnant women everywhere.

Of all of the millions of stimuli that bombard you, your built-in filter system decides what you will notice and give attention to and what you will ignore. Less than 1 percent of the stimuli that hit you every single day from every angle get through to your conscious mind, because the filters screen and block out everything that is not relevant to what you are focused on at that moment.

*You **lock on** to the information that you consider valuable, and you **lock out** information you do not perceive as valuable.*

The trick is making sure you are locking on to the right stuff and locking out the wrong stuff.

This is why having a compelling goal is so important. Once you make the decision that something is really important to you, any information that will help you achieve that goal will become clear.

More and more, as you focus on your goal, dream, or desire, your subconscious mind will accept it as something worthy of its attention. Once accepted, instead of working to maintain the status quo, your subconscious mind will begin to recognize and collect all of the data required to bring your goal to pass. This often occurs in ways that seem miraculous.

Garbage In, Garbage Out

Out of the 99 percent of the stimuli and information that is screened out by your mind's filter, there is the possibility that a lot of the information could help you accomplish your goals. There is also the possibility that the 1 percent you are focusing on isn't the right focus. Remember, your conscious mind sets the goal, but it is your subconscious mind that helps you get the information to attain your goal. Your subconscious mind supplies your conscious mind with screened information, so your behavior is only as wise as the information that is provided.

Your actions and decisions are dependent on the quality of information that your subconscious mind brings forth.

Bad information results in bad actions and decisions.

Plant a Garden

Your subconscious mind is a lot like soil, which is nonjudgmental— whatever you plant there will grow. It won't judge you or complain about what you plant. If you plant seeds of grass, you get grass. If you plant seeds of roses, you get roses.

When you plant positive intentions in your subconscious mind, your mind garden flourishes, but if you leave it unattended or allow negative thoughts to creep in, weeds will sprout. Like with your front yard, where I am sure you haven't deliberately planted weeds, if you are not intentional with your thoughts and don't monitor what thoughts are coming in, all kinds of ideas can fall into the soil. And as soon as they fall, they take root and grow.

What you are experiencing right now in your life is the result of the seeds—good or bad—that you have planted in the past.

If you want to change your experience, you need to plant something new in your subconscious mind. The good news is that it isn't necessary to pull every single weed out. As you plant new and improved seeds, you can overwhelm your garden with healthy strong roots that overshadow and eventually kill the weeds, because there is not enough room for the weeds to thrive. Not only will the weeds die, but they won't come back because there simply isn't any room for them any more.

Your brain works the same way, because your external world is always a byproduct of your internal world. You must change on the inside and plant new seeds in your subconscious mind in order to create long-lasting change. You get to decide what information and stimuli have value, and what you determine has value gets through to your subconscious mind.

Don't concern yourself with things that don't hold value and that don't contribute to your success.

For example, the opinions of others are not your business. Stay focused on the opinion that you hold of yourself.

What weeds are lingering in your mind garden? What new thoughts can you plant to begin the process of changing your mind?

*And be not conformed to this world: but be
ye transformed by the renewing of your mind, that
ye may prove what is that good, and acceptable,
and perfect, will of God.*
—Romans 12:2

REFLECTIONS

- Your willpower always fights a losing battle against your belief system.

- Your mind has three distinct parts that make up the thought process:

  ○ Conscious mind
  ○ Subconscious mind
  ○ Creative subconscious mind

- Goal-setting is a conscious act, whereas goal attainment is a subconscious act.

- Your actions and decisions are only as wise as the information they are based on.

- You lock on to the information that you consider valuable, and you lock out information you do not perceive as valuable.

SELF-DISCOVERY QUESTIONS

1. What past "truths" or ideas may be stored in your subconscious that may impact your behavior, outlook, or performance today?

2. Where might you have "blind spots" in your life now?

3. Have you ever been so sure about something that you completely ignored evidence to the contrary?

THE POWER OF ATTITUDE

"The power of life and death are in the tongue…"
Proverbs 18:21

What do you say when you talk to yourself? Do you encourage yourself or are you overly critical?

*Self-talk is defined as my own words that trigger **pictures, emotions,** and **feelings** that result in my attitude (self-image) about myself.*

Do you pay attention to how you talk to yourself? Are there certain words you use consistently when describing yourself? A great question to ask yourself regarding your self-talk is, "Would you allow someone else to talk to you the way you talk to you?" If someone else called you "stupid," your feelings would be hurt and/or whoever called you that would be in for a fight. Yet when you call yourself "stupid," you consider it to be okay?

> *"Would you allow someone else to talk to you the way you talk to you?"*

The truth is that you believe what you say to yourself *more* than what everyone else says about you. Therefore, you need to make sure that what you are repeating to yourself is what you want to see in your life.

Attitudes are formed by words that trigger pictures, which then bring upon *emotions*, which then predict or perpetuate performance. These pictures bring your words to life.

For example, when you think of the word "success," what pictures do you see? As soon as you read that sentence, your mind immediately connected that word with pictures you have stored in your conscious and subconscious mind—perhaps pictures of successful people who you know, money, a business suit, a happy family, good health, vacations, or a dream home came to mind.

All of the pictures in your mind associated with the word "success" came to the forefront, and these pictures brought emotions. How did you feel when you saw these pictures in your mind? Did you feel happy? Did you feel sad because you don't see yourself associated with the word "success"? I know you felt something because emotions run deep. That is the reason why your words are so powerful.

Without emotion, words and pictures lack impact. This is why seeing statistics about children who are hungry has less of an impact than seeing pictures or meeting them.

We change the most when we are shown a truth that influences our feelings versus a fact analysis that shifts our thinking. We can't emotionally connect to a number, but we can definitely connect with a picture or person.

Maya Angelou taught us, "We may not remember what people say, but we remember how people make us feel." The deeper the emotion, the longer it is remembered and recorded in your subconscious mind.

Your self-talk is your internal advertising campaign. What are you advertising about yourself? Are there certain words that you could use more of? Are you currently using "killer phrases," meaning, are there certain phrases that are negative, critical, or judgmental?

Powerful self-talk consists of good "put-ups." Avoid put-downs as you talk to yourself. Pay attention to the conversations that you have with yourself, as well as conversations that you have with others.

There is a language of success; there is a language of distress. There is a language of progress, and there is a language of regress. Words sell, words repel. Words lead, words impede. Words heal, words kill. How do you use your words?
—Stephen R. Covey

Another term for self-talk is *affirmation*.

Affirmations are statements of fact or belief about reality as you perceive it right now; they shape self-esteem and self-image and control performance. Your affirmations form your attitude.

In Chapter Nine, we will dive into great detail about how to selectively choose affirmations that are in alignment with your goals to reprogram your subconscious mind. You will learn how to use your affirmations to your advantage and allow them to work for you, not against you. For now, it is important to understand how your current self-talk is shaping your self-image and self-esteem and forming your attitudes.

Realize that you hold the power of life and death in your tongue. We've already discussed how your subconscious mind cannot differentiate between a real experience and an imagined experience. Use this to your advantage! Your words automatically trigger pictures. You can't stop it, but you can use it to your benefit.

You are constantly affirming who you are—for better or worse. So, what if you begin to use words with emotion that create new beliefs? Once you put this new information into your subconscious, you can act out that new belief that contains the right attitudes, knowledge, and skills. Your words will generate positive pictures, and thus bring on positive emotions.

> *Realize that you hold the power of life and death in your tongue.*

We know that negative emotions can feel more powerful than positive ones, so you need to be very careful with what you imagine. Choose positive self-talk regardless of what you are actually experiencing in real life. Your positive words will create a positive picture that triggers a positive emotion, and thus creates a positive outcome.

Words are not true or false. They are simply tools that can be used to build or destroy. Are we using our words to build life or create death? In our marriage, are we talking about avoiding a divorce or creating a healthy marriage? Are we talking about avoiding poverty or creating financial freedom and abundance?

Before I keynote, I picture it going well and getting applause at the end. I hear the clapping every single time before I step on stage.

When I'm speaking, I focus on the people in the audience who are engaged and excited about my presentation. If I were to focus on those who have their arms folded and appear to be disengaged, it would shake my confidence and shift my focus negatively.

Which Way Are You Leaning?

The right attitude is *everything*. Individuals who succeed against overwhelming odds have one thing in common: a great attitude.

*Your attitude is the direction in which you **lean** at the subconscious level. It is a habit of thinking that is stored in your subconscious mind. It controls your spontaneous actions.*

Your attitude is formed by your affirmations or self-talk. A good attitude is not walking around with a smile on your face, denying reality. It is not pretending everything is okay. Instead, your attitude is a tangible variable that plays a significant part in every outcome of your life.

> *Your attitude is the direction in which you* lean *at the subconscious level.*

In every aspect of our lives, there is an event, a response, and an outcome. Jack Canfield describes it as E (event) + R (response, which is dictated by your attitude) = O (outcome). *Outcomes vary based on your response to the event.* Your attitude is either a multiplier or a divider of your greatness.

Your attitude has a significant impact because it multiplies or divides your greatness. Your skills and knowledge enhance your greatness, but your attitude is the multiplier or divider.

> *Any fact facing us is not as important as our attitude toward it, for that determines our success or failure.*
> —Norman Vincent Peale

Changing your attitude is not as simple as putting a smile on your face. It is all about choice. Our attitudes are a habit of thinking, and habits are created by choice. In order to change your attitude, you must choose to change the words that you use toward yourself and others. It is a rigorous process of thought redirection.

Attitudes are formed three-dimensionally through your words, which trigger pictures, which bring about emotions.

When you change your words, your pictures and emotions change automatically. The law of attraction states that you move toward and become like that which is held uppermost in your mind, so direct your words in the direction you want your life to go.

As a leader, coach in the direction you want your team to go. Words are powerful tools in doing this, because they predict or perpetuate performance. Words are your tool to make change happen.

Direct your words in the direction you want your life to go.

Another way of speaking is how you present yourself, because your body language plays a significant role in how you communicate. Research indicates that less than 10 percent of communication between people is in words and over 90 percent is body language, as well as vocal tone and inflection.

When we communicate with each other, our ability to connect has to do with matching our pictures, not just our words. We may be *saying* the same thing but not *picturing* the same thing. We don't truly communicate until our pictures match. What is said doesn't drive the outcome—what is pictured does.

When it comes to sorting words, there are words that carry a lot of power and some that don't matter at all. Choose words that uplift and inspire yourself and others.

Train to Be Great

To be honest, I am not the biggest fan of New Year's resolutions. Instead of calling it a resolution and trying your best to make the change, I would rather see you transform it into a goal and *train* yourself to make the change. As a result, the goal becomes an expectation.

Expectations influence your behavior and create long-lasting change. When you create expectations for yourself, you don't try to get in shape, be a better spouse, or become a better parent; you *train* to be those things.

When you just "try," you don't commit. So when you experience a setback, you are ready to quit or start over again.

One day a man walked up to me at the gym and said, "Tell me about one of your workouts. I am not satisfied with my results." We spoke for a few minutes, then I asked him how long he had been working out.

"Three weeks," he said.

Three weeks? I took a few moments to regain my composure. Not only was he insulting me, but also every other person in the gym who had been consistently coming to the gym for a long time!

The lesson here is that seeking to change and be great isn't about "getting a new workout." I need you to *train* and stay committed to the MTG plan you are already working on.

Don't Drop the Ball

I'll never forget one of my first games as a rookie with the New York Jets. I was lined up at the line of scrimmage for a third and long pass play. I was nervous. The quarterback called out the play, "Blue 15, blue 15…", which meant the ball was most likely coming to me. I kept repeating to myself, *Don't drop the ball! Don't drop the ball!*

Let's break this down to the attitude level. Our subconscious mind sees in pictures. Because the word "don't" doesn't have a picture associated with it, my mind doesn't hear *Don't*, but it does hear, *Drop the ball.* What pictures do the words "drop the ball" trigger? Of course— dropping the ball. What emotions are created from mental pictures of dropping the ball? Failure. Disappointment. Embarrassment.

Here I am standing at the line of scrimmage, the play hasn't even started yet and in my mind, I have already failed. As my thoughts continue, now not only have I dropped the ball in my mind, but I have been reprimanded by my coach and cut from the team! Remember, all this has happened before the play while I am still standing at the line of scrimmage.

In my conscious mind, I am telling myself, *Don't drop the ball,* which feels like I have control, but my subconscious mind (which is far more powerful than my conscious mind) locks on to the picture. At this point, my creative subconscious mind goes to work. Remember, its job is to "resolve conflict," creatively problem solve, and make sure I "act like me." It gathers all of my previous experiences of actually dropping the ball and makes that its goal. Its job is to make sure that my external world and my internal belief match whether or not the outcome is positive or negative. It is up to me to ensure that what I am affirming is what I want to see in my life. This is why we must be intentional with our words. Casualness can lead to casualties. This is the Law of Mental Equivalency.

Of course, I am not trying to fail, but because I am attempting to avoid failure instead of focusing on success, I gravitate toward failure. Any guesses on how my story ends?

The ball is snapped and I run my route. The quarterback sees that I am wide open. He throws, and the ball comes at me in what feels like slow motion. I reach up, the ball hits my hands, and drops. *Yikes!* The home crowd erupts—and a whole stadium of fans boo me off the field.

This incident wasn't a skill or talent issue. There was no excuse for me to drop the ball. Based on the size of my hands alone, I should have just reached up and grabbed it out of the air with one hand.

Because of my self-talk, though, it was a self-fulfilling prophecy to drop the ball. I told my mind what to do, and it went to work to accomplish the goal. Instead of telling myself to drop the ball, what if I had just flipped it? What if as I was standing on the line of scrimmage, I had told myself, *Make a big play. Catch the ball. Snatch it out of the air. Score!* What if I had locked on to the positive picture instead of a negative one? My subconscious and creative subconscious minds would have worked together just as effectively to make catching the ball part of my external experience.

It is that simple. By locking on the positive, we raise our probability of succees.

Your words are extremely powerful. They begin the process of how your attitudes are formed and maintained. Remember, attitudes are the multiplier or divider of your greatness. If I work with people who are convinced they can succeed, I can lower the relative importance of their skillset.

The need for skills or knowledge isn't as valuable as the need for a positive, winning attitude.

Words either build or destroy. How are you using your words? Are you building a successful future or destroying it?

*I wonder if there is really anything more important when
it comes to monitoring your attitude than monitoring the
way you talk to you about you and your potential.*
—Unknown

How do you talk to yourself? Do you build yourself up with your
words or tear yourself down? Do you remember that your subconscious mind is completely nonjudgmental? It accepts whatever you
feed it. It cannot tell the difference between a real experience and a
vividly imagined experience accompanied
with emotion—to the degree that you vividly imagine the event. You can become
mentally experienced at an event before it
takes place! When you use your imagination, the experience is stored in your subconscious mind as "truth and reality" and
will be later be used as true information.

*Words either build
or destroy. How
are you using
your words? Are
you building a
successful future or
destroying it?*

My experience in dropping the football
is an indicator of what happens when your
subconscious mind is used in a negative way.
Your self-talk, another way to describe affirmations, either builds you
up or tears you down. It either inspires or destroys. The word "inspire"
means "to breathe life into." Your words can breathe life into your
goals, breathe life into your dreams, and breathe life into your very life.

Wherever your heart is, your treasure will be also.

The Power of Focus

One of your greatest gifts is the ability to focus. When Tiger Woods
was at his prime, all he could see was the hole. As a child, his dad had
taught him to visualize a picture above the hole and to hit the picture.
When Tiger looked at the hole, it wasn't a hole in the ground, but rather
it was a picture above it. He would always putt to the picture. This was
a powerful habit that engaged his subconscious and creative subconscious minds. For Tiger, the benefit of hitting the picture translated
into hundreds of millions of dollars.

Similarly, as a wide receiver in football, the picture you want to
see with a laser-like focus is the tip of the ball: *See the tip; find the tip;*

catch the tip. If you see the tip of the football, you can grab the rest of the football. Your mind can't concentrate on two things at once, so if you focus on the tip of the ball, your fear and worry disappear. If you don't focus on the tip, then your mind gets distracted by the fears, worry, and anxiety. That increases the probability that you won't catch the ball. *Feelings follow focus!*

> *Feelings follow focus!*

Focus is a simple action with a huge return.

Do you see how these examples relate to your life? Do you keep your focus on the right things?

"It Is an Issue of Focus"

There are aspects of your life that are true—even important—but not that critical, because you can't do anything about them. You just can't change everything in your life, so it is important that you focus on what you can do and where you have control.

To improve your attitude, you must shift your focus to what is working in your life.

Ask yourself what is working and how you can create more of this success. Shine a light on your successes and put 100 percent of your focus on the percentage of your life that is working.

It is all about focus.

Wayne Gretzky, one of the greatest hockey players of all time, was once asked, "Wayne, what is the difference between a fifty-goal scorer and a five-goal scorer?"

Wayne responded, "You know, attitude is not really talent. The difference is a fifty-goal scorer, they're so clear, their focus is simply on the back of the net. That is all they see. Where the five-goal scorer, they can tell you the name brand of every pad of every goalie in the league. I see the back of the net, they see the goalie."

Low performers see what they don't want to have happen and dwell on past losses. High performers see what they want to have happen and dwell on past wins.

It is all in how you see it. Do you see an opportunity in every difficulty or difficulty in every opportunity?

Stop the Complain Train

Because words are so powerful, you must be aware of the impact complaining has on the people around you.

Attitudes are contagious, and your words are the mechanism that allows attitudes to spread.

Complaining is unique, because instead of bringing focus, it searches for more justification for what is being complained about. You feed it, and it grows.

Jack Canfield said it best: "The problem with complaining is people rarely complain to someone who can do something about it. We complain about our spouse at work. We complain about our coworkers at home. And just get nervous at the Christmas party that they run into each other."

Complaining has a destructive power that destroys everything in its path. When you complain, you are spitting out words and creating pictures that bring negative emotions.

Sometimes we have opinions of people whom we have never met and problems with things that have never happened to us. We create these inaccurate stories about situations where we were never involved.

Attitudes are contagious, and your words are the mechanism that allow attitudes to spread. This means fear is contagious, but so is courage. Negativity is contagious, but so is positivity.

*Don't just use your words to **describe** the situation. Use your words to **change** the situation.*

When you make the decision to stop complaining, your happiness, joy, contentment, peace, and appreciation immediately increase fifty-fold. If you do nothing else to accomplish MTG, stop complaining! You will start feeling better because feelings are a lagging indicator. Feelings follow focus and because your focus is on something positive, inspiring, and goal-oriented, your feelings will start coinciding with that.

Instead of complaining, make a request or suggestion. There is no reason to have a conversation with a person who can't do anything about what you are complaining about. For example, it makes little sense to complain about your spouse at work and your coworkers at home.

The reason why you choose to talk to someone who can't do anything about it is because this helps you feel better about yourself in the moment, but it does not solve the problem.

Instead, go directly to the source and make a request.

One of the benefits of going directly to the source is that you feel empowered instead of avoiding the issue. Stop complaining about the problem that you permit! When you complain, you continue to live in the problem. When you address it, you begin to live in the solution.

Are You a Marionette Doll?

Instead of living in the problem with a negative attitude, you must bring the problem up, find the solution, and then live positively in the solution. Everything you do is then invested in that solution.

The challenge is that your perception is 95 percent subjective in any situation—influenced by every past experience, what you have heard, what you have read, and what you have been told. The 5 percent that is objective often doesn't come into play because your subjectivity is so powerful. You literally can become a marionette doll that is controlled by every influence of your past.

Use your attitude to cut the strings. Use new words to create new pictures that trigger new emotions. Take control of your life and create new outcomes.

Are you ready to cut those marionette strings and unleash your greatness?

If you spend 100 percent of your time thinking about the 10 percent in your life that isn't working, you will feel horrible.

Attitude Is the Happiness Factor

For most people, perhaps only about 10 percent of their life that isn't "right" but they spend 100 percent of their time thinking about what is "wrong." If you spend 100 percent of your time thinking about the 10 percent in your life that isn't working, you will feel horrible. Or you could have only 1 percent of your life that isn't right, but if you spend 100 percent of your thinking about that 1 percent, you feel just as bad as if 10 percent of your life wasn't right!

Do you see where I am going with this? What if you changed your focus? What if you focused 100 percent of your time on the 90 percent that is working in your life?

You can learn from the 10 percent in your life that's not going well. But that must not be your focus.

Studies have shown that when the lives of happy people and sad people are studied, both groups have similar life circumstances. Both happy and sad people experience stress, divorce, financial difficulty, death of loved ones, illness, and other challenges.

Maxwell Maltz, the author of *Psycho-Cybernetics*, states that happiness is really a state of mind where your thoughts are pleasant the majority of the time.

Happiness is a result of a person's attitude, not the life circumstances.

Coach Yourself Forward

When I give a keynote speech, I seek feedback on what might help me improve my presentation, but I focus on the kind of feedback that will actually benefit me and "coach me forward" versus the kind of feedback or negativity that will coach me backward. I want feedback on where I want to go, not on what I want to avoid.

As a leader, are you coaching people toward the solution or back to the problem?

> *You don't change performance by*
> *pointing out where people are.*
> —Unknown

To coach forward, you first remind the people around you of their true identity and then offer feedback. This principle is great for parenting, too, and I have used it with my daughters.

As a leader, are you coaching people toward the solution or back to the problem?

For example, with my daughter, Madison, there were a few days when she wasn't telling the truth and I had to call her on it. I had to be careful, because everything in me wanted to say, "You are a liar! What's wrong with you? Don't be lying like that!" But instead, with the same intensity and passion, I shifted my focus to her identity.

The first words out of my mouth were, "This is not who you are. This is not like you. Are you kidding me? You are so much bigger and better than this; this is not Madison!" I reaffirmed her significance and value, then addressed the problem. It made her feel, *You are right, Dad. That isn't me.*

As you reflect on the people around you, ask yourself:

- Am I coaching people forward or coaching them backward?
- Do my words inspire (breathe life into) their dreams and goals, or do my words cause people's dreams and goals to expire and cease to exist?

This same principle applies to how you talk to yourself. You must make sure that your words build you up and coach you forward. Pay attention to how you describe and talk to yourself.

Affirm your potential and your success. Don't affirm your failures and disappointments.

Retrospective Feedback

Watching film is a major part of performance improvement in football, as well as other sports. Watching film allows the coach to introduce objective feedback, but at some point, the instruction hits a plateau. And the plateau is less about the objectivity or effectiveness of the film; it is more about the skill level of the coaches giving the feedback.

When the coaches use the film to correct a player's performance, if they don't know how to correct properly, they can create bigger problems. For example, if the coach spends too much time on the player's mistakes versus how he can succeed, the negative performance becomes the focus, and there is little improvement. The feedback coaches the player backward toward the problem instead of forward toward the solution.

We all need just enough feedback to course correct. Anything beyond what went wrong and how to correct it is counterproductive.

Another problem that could be created when watching film is if the coaches leave the discussion of a failed play without telling the player what *better* looks like. To coach a player forward, it is necessary to paint a clear picture of what should have happened. If an alternative isn't given, the players really don't know any better and will probably continue doing the same thing.

"Not on My Watch"

One day during one of my college football games, I made a mistake. I fumbled and lost the football to our opponent, and coach Mike Dunbar got angry—I mean, really angry. He lit into me with a cuss word, ended with a cuss word, and strung together a lot more cuss words in the middle that didn't really fit together. His anger wasn't just about my mistake as much as it was about my nonchalant attitude toward my mistake.

I remember kneeling down to one knee with my head down, and tears began to well up in my eyes. I had never been ripped apart by a coach like that. I knew that I had messed up, but I did not think that this level of punishment fit the crime. As he continued his tirade into me, there was something he said that changed everything for me.

"You have so much talent and so much ability. You have the talent to be playing football on Sundays [in the NFL], and my goal is to make sure that happens. I will not allow you to waste your talent on my watch. Greatness is in you, and I am going to get it out of you even if it kills *you!*"

Coach Dunbar could cuss at me all he wanted to help me improve, but it might not have mattered if he had not affirmed me and my potential. Once he affirmed what he saw in me that changed how I received his feedback. It no longer felt like he was coaching me backward, but he was now coaching me forward. He corrected my behavior in alignment with my identity and potential. I knew he truly cared about me.

I am not suggesting that he did not need to work on his people management skills, but I gave him permission to coach me as hard as necessary. He spoke to not only my head, but also to my heart.

Dr. John Kotter, an international authority on leadership from Harvard University, states, "Our main finding put simply is that behavior change happens successfully only by speaking to people's feelings (heart)."

Coach Dunbar found a way to help me see the problem in ways that influenced my emotions, not just my thoughts. His method of feedback did not change, but the *meaning* behind his feedback changed. Once he affirmed what he knew I could become, all the cussing, yelling, and screaming felt different. I knew the feedback was *for me*, not against me.

He was speaking to the *greatness in me*, not the weakness in me.

> *Continuously remind your team of what they are capable of becoming.*

As leaders, this is how we coach our people forward. We always want to give feedback, especially difficult feedback, in the context of what we believe our prople can become. Continuously remind your team of what they are capable of becoming.

Who has spoken to the greatness in you? Who have you coached forward?

There Is Hope

My mentor, Bob Moawad, has advised me that high performers dwell on what they want to have happen and think about or focus on past wins. Low performers dwell on what they don't want to happen and focus on past losses. That is the biggest difference between a high and low performer.

Always make a conscious decision to align your words with the goal you want to accomplish and the direction you want to move in, not with what you want to avoid.

You are in charge of how you talk to yourself. No one else can have this conversation—it's completely up to you—and that is the good news! When you take control of your attitude by taking control of your self-talk, you begin to take control of your life!

Pay attention to your words, and you'll gain control of your performance. Make the choice to improve your self-talk today. The minute you believe that your life is your own, you begin to live.

REFLECTIONS

- An attitude is the direction in which you *lean* at the subconscious level.

- Our subconscious mind cannot tell the difference between a real experience and a vividly imagined experience accompanied by emotion.

- We can predict the performance we don't want to have happen.

- Words can be used to build or destroy.

- You don't improve performance by pointing out where people are failing.

- High Performers

  - See what they *want* to have happen.
  - Dwell on past wins.

- Low Performers

  - See what they *don't want* to have happen.
  - Dwell on past losses.

- Attitudes are formed three-dimensionally through your words, which trigger pictures that bring about emotions.

- The power of life and death is in the tongue.

- Attitudes are contagious, and your words are the mechanism that allows attitudes to spread.

- To improve your attitude, you must shift your focus to what is working in your life.

SELF-DISCOVERY QUESTIONS

1. What is your self-talk in the different areas of your life? (Family, friendships, career, health, finances, spiritual life, recreation, etc.)

2. Can words kill? Can a look kill? Not with a knife or with a gun, but with a sigh and a roll of the eyes?

6

SELF-IMAGE EXPLORED

I Am a Millionaire

While speaking at the National Association of Realtors in New Orleans, I met a man who had recently lost over $30 million in real estate investments. This was back in 2009, shortly after the real estate market bubble popped.

He said to me, "Eric, we probably only have about 40 percent of the attendees here this year compared to last year. When we have a crisis like we just experienced, only the pros remain."

"I see why," I said.

"It is totally understandable," he added. "It is not that I just lost $30 million; I was on the positive end of $30 million. I tried to hold on to things, so now I am in the negative for millions of dollars as well. If I were at zero, that would be awesome."

Wow, he was underneath zero and looking up.

He continued, "I was concerned, but now I have owned it and realize where I am. I'm not a millionaire because of real estate. I'm a millionaire because I have a millionaire mind. The method that I just happened to use was real estate. There's all kinds of ways I can be a millionaire."

What a great attitude! Lo and behold, two years later this same gentleman was at the same conference speaking about how he had recovered and the process followed to get back on top! What is amazing is that he experienced the same circumstances that so many others had, but he found a way to thrive again. He was a millionaire in his mind, even when his bank account didn't reflect it. He found the money, and the money found him.

Now the opposite is also true. It's reported that over 70 percent of lottery winners end up broke within five years after they win. A reason for this is their *self-image*. They have a million dollars in the bank but not a millionaire mindset. They make inappropriate actions and decisions that lead to the loss of all the money they gained. Externally, they just happened to win millions of dollars but internally, their self-image was screaming, "This isn't who you are! You were lucky!"

Self-Image—Your Achievement Regulator

Your self-image is your achievement regulator. It is the accumulation of your thought patterns throughout your life that you have about yourself—real as well as imagined. It is what you believe to be true about yourself, how you see yourself.

You will never perform consistently higher than the level of your self-image, which continually monitors who you are and how you behave based on your affirmations (self-talk).

*Another way of describing your self-image is that it's a complex picture of what you **believe** you are capable of, who you **believe** you are, and what you **believe** you deserve.*

Your self-image controls your attitudes, your abilities, your income level, your patience, your opportunities, and more.

> *Success is not to be pursued; it is to be attracted*
> *by the person we become.*
> —Jim Rohn

The original meaning of the word "deserve" was "of service." You can't have success at a discount. You *know* you deserve something based on either the fact that you paid the "cost" for it or you put in the work.

This mindset is very different from feeling entitled. Entitlement is the belief that you inherently deserve something without any effort.

Feeling entitled hinders your ability to put yourself in the right mind-set to deserve, or be *ready to receive* what you want.

For example, when we give something to someone who didn't earn it or doesn't believe they are worthy, internally their self-image screams, "It's not mine; I don't deserve it!" So when they get it, they sabotage it. This is why lotteries and unexpected large inheritances can be so stressful for families.

I asked a friend of mine who is an accountant, "In your line of work, when is the most stressful time for people?"

His answer: "Eric, I deal with couples who have been married for over thirty years and get an inheritance they didn't anticipate. Suddenly the money creates problems in their marriage they never could have imagined. You'd think that the money showing up would solve the problems, not create them."

> *For example, when we give something to someone who didn't earn it or doesn't believe they are worthy, internally their self-image screams, "It's not mine; I don't deserve it!" So when they get it, they sabotage it.*

The reason is that regardless of whether it is good or bad, the extra money is inconsistent with their self-image. Remember, your creative subconscious mind's job is to make sure your external world and internal world match, and your internal image is much more powerful than the external world. Your external world is simply a reflection of what's going on internally.

If internally your self-image is saying, "I'm always in debt. I live paycheck to paycheck," even if you get a raise, you will find a way to still live paycheck to paycheck.

Does your self-image match what you truly want to experience in life?

Comfort Zone

Your comfort zone is the range of performance where you feel the most comfortable; it is the zone that corresponds with your current, dominant self-image. When you perform outside of your comfort zone, including higher or lower performance:

1. You get anxiety and tension feedback;
2. You recreate the conditions that existed in your comfort zone. In other words, "You get back to where you belong."

Prison of the Mind

A man who that had been incarcerated for twenty-two of his thirty-six years was released from prison. Finally, he was free to move forward with his life.

A few months as a free man went by and he was having trouble adjusting to his new life on the other side of the bars. He decided to rob a store, but instead of running with the cash, he waited for the police to arrive. *He wanted to be caught.*

When he had his day in court, he told the judge, "Your honor, I just want to get this over with and get back home."

Ouch! In his mind, home was…prison. He did not see himself as a free man, but instead saw himself as an inmate who temporarily was away from home. Remember, any time we are outside of our comfort zone (above or below it), we get anxiety and tension feedback. We also recreate the conditions that allow us to get back to where we are comfortable, even though we have the potential to do so much more.

I have worked with the Department of Corrections in my home state of Washington serving both men and women who have been incarcerated. My goal has been to help them raise their self-image to match where they are going versus where they have been. While working at one of the facilities, the warden mentioned that they receive phone calls from released inmates asking if they can come back. That's the power of comfort zones!

This is an extreme example, but we all have hidden prisons in our mind. The good news is that we no longer have to remain in them; we have the keys to get out!

The "V" illustration which follows represents your *potential* in any area of your life: family, friends, career, health, community, spirituality, finance, or recreation. Your self-image—what you believe to be true about yourself—is on the left. As the illustration shows, your self-image is the cause, and your comfort zone is the effect. Too often people attempt to change using willpower: "I am going to change even if it kills me!"

As I mentioned in Chapter Four, willpower comes in second to your belief system. It is not a fair fight. So doesn't it make more sense to raise your self-image? This is what I describe as changing from the inside out. As your self-image rises, your comfort zone has no recourse but to rise as well.

The "I Can Become" zone represents what you are capable of—a goal, dream, or possibility. To achieve and maintain that goal, you must raise your comfort zone. And the only way you can raise your comfort zone is by raising your self-image. Do you see how this works?

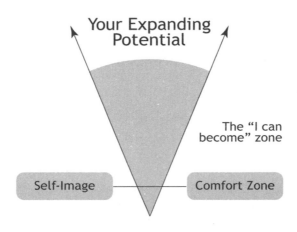

This "V" represents your expanding potential and effectiveness in any area of your life.

Lying on Nails

The issue with a comfort zone is that it has nothing to do with what you are capable of. Reaching a new goal or level of success is not an issue of potential, but rather an issue of what you believe about yourself. Comfort zones are established based on where you feel most confident. It doesn't matter that you don't like your comfort zone. All that matters is that you are *comfortable* in it. You may even complain about it, but it's yours. It is that level of certainty and comfort that keeps you there.

This is why it's easier for a major crisis to move you out of your comfort zone than a slightly unpleasant experience that you can adapt to. The crisis forces you to change out of necessity. However, if you can adapt to something, you will simply learn how to incorporate it into your comfort zone and live with it.

To illustrate this, there was a gentleman who went to visit an old farmer he knew. They were sitting on the porch when the visitor noticed his dog lying on a nail. He asked the old farmer, "Sir, why is your dog lying on the nail?" The old farmer replied, "Because it's not sharp enough."

He nailed it. (No pun intended!) The dog simply adapted to the nail because it wasn't a big enough problem for him to change his comfort zone. The dog liked his spot on the porch and a dull nail wasn't going to make him move.

What nails are you lying on? Are there problems in your life that you have learned to live with?

> *The chains of habit are too weak to be felt until*
> *they are too strong to be broken.*
> —Unknown

NFL—Not For Long

When I got drafted by the New York Jets and then eventually played for the Green Bay Packers, my coaches told me how much talent I had, and they invested in my improvement. But even though I was dressed up in a New York Jets or a Green Bay Packers uniform, in my heart I was still a wide receiver for Central Washington University. In my head, I questioned my ability and felt like I didn't deserve to play in the NFL.

My self-talk went like this: *I'm a receiver from Central Washington University. That's who I really am. I don't belong here. Am I really capable of doing this? Do I even deserve it? I mean, there are other guys who I know are better than me who aren't here, and here I am.* Everything in me was screaming, "You don't deserve this!" And guess what happened? It wasn't long before I found myself out of the league. I could blame the torn ligaments in my knee, my strained shoulder, or torn calf muscle, but in truth my self-image (confidence in myself) never caught up. It was my talent and potential that kept me in the league for those three years.

One of my teammates, Terrence Mathis, was the opposite of me. He had a self-image that I admired. Terrence is a smaller guy, about 5'10", but he had an amazing attitude and a strong self-image. Every day his body language said, *I am a playmaker. I am one of the best receivers out here. I make plays every time I am on the field.*

Now from a physical standpoint, I was much bigger than Terrence. At the time, I was 6'3" and 220 pounds. I was fast with long arms and giant hands, but my physical talent could not make up for a self-defeating attitude. Terrence had physical talent, and his strong self-image maximized it even more. Terrence played for over eleven years in the NFL and had a very successful career.

What do you think the difference was between him and me? Was it ability? Talent? No, it was his *self-image*. What he believed to be true about himself was different than what I believed to be true about myself. He not only believed that he deserved to be in the NFL, but also that he would thrive in the NFL. I didn't.

You will never rise higher than the image that you have of yourself, even though you have all the potential in the world.

What do you believe to be true about yourself?

You will never rise higher than the image that you have of yourself, even though you have all the potential in the world.

Your self-image doesn't *define* your potential, but it certainly can *limit* your potential because it corresponds with your comfort zone. This limitation can create feelings of dissatisfaction and stagnancy, but it is important to understand that feeling stagnant or stuck isn't a *passive* response.

You didn't fall victim to feeling that way. Rather, you feel that way because you are *actively resisting a change to your comfort zone*. If you open yourself up and begin to change your self-image, the feelings of dissatisfaction and stagnancy will dissipate.

Your self-image and comfort zone restrict you to levels that feel familiar. The good news is that this principle is neutral and works in both directions. This means that if you improve your self-image and expand your comfort zone, you will immediately begin to move toward your desired level of performance.

You can create positive changes by following this principle. Of course, you can allow your comfort zone to stay the same, but I challenge you to do the work to expand it. Appendix B is a Self-Image Survey. This exercise allows you to identify vulnerabilities in your self-image. You will identify which beliefs are holding you back from expanding your comfort zone and accomplishing your goals.

How Do You Get from Where You Are to Where You Want to Be?

When I ask the question, "How do you get from where you are to where you want to be?" the majority of the answers I receive can be summed up in one word—motivation.

"I just need to be more motivated," they say. I often get this answer from leaders, managers, coaches, and parents, yet *we are always motivated.* Motivation ("motive-action") is what you would rather do than not do at any given time. It is monitored by your dominant attitude and self-image. Raise your self-image, raise your motivation.

There are three different types of motivation: restrictive (fear), incentive, and attitude. Let's dive in to the characteristics of all three types.

Restrictive motivation is negative, extrinsic, and temporary. Restrictive motivation is created by fear. It is autocratic, dictatorial, and often threatening. It works if the fear is great enough. When restrictive (fear) motivation is used, the message is, "I'm incompetent." There is no personal accountability and very little dignity for those involved. Restrictive motivation does *not* have a positive impact on your self-image. We learn to either get used to it or get away from it. Despite its negative results, restrictive motivation is still often used.

On the flip side, incentive motivation is positive, extrinsic, and temporary. It is positive rather than negative, but it too is extrinsic and temporary. When we are motivated with incentives, we fall in love with the reward, not the activity.

What does that mean? It means that last year's reward becomes this year's right. Rewards usually need to get bigger, better, and/or different to remain effective. In my professional playing days, we called this the "winner's disease."

If your motivation is driven by the rewards of the game more than your love of the game, winning will be a temporary experience instead of a consistent experience. Once the goal is reached, motivation dissipates. When one truly loves the game, the winning takes care of itself.

This is why the focus of MTG is on attitude motivation.

Attitude motivation is the most effective method of motivation, because it is based on clearly defined pay-value (benefit) plus deep personal satisfaction.

It is positive, long-lasting, and intrinsic. Love of the activity is fundamental.

The key to effectively motivating yourself and others is to foster change from the inside out. This inside-out change that we are focused on is changing your self-image.

Turn Up Your Internal Thermostat

Your self-image regulates your level of performance similar to the way a thermostat regulates the temperature in a room. When the temperature on the thermostat is set at 72 degrees, it also provides a "comfort zone" that allows the temperature to move up to 74 degrees or down to 70 degrees. If the temperature in the room drops below 70 degrees, the heating system kicks in to move the temperature back up into the range that has been programmed on the thermostat. If the temperature rises above 74 degrees, the cooling system kicks in to move the temperature back down into the preferred range. The thermostat's electrical signals continue to respond to changes in either direction in order to keep the temperature in the desired range.

Similarly, you have an internal psychological thermostat (self-image) that regulates your performance. Instead of electrical signals, your self-image uses discomfort signals to keep you within your comfort zone. If your behavior approaches the edge of your comfort zone, you begin to feel uncomfortable and anxious. If what you are experiencing is outside the self-image that you unconsciously hold, your body will send signals of mental tension and physical discomfort to your system. To avoid the discomfort, you unconsciously pull yourself back into your comfort zone.

Being stuck in a comfort zone does not mean you are not moving—it means you are spinning. The cooling and heating system of your internal thermostat is working hard to keep you in your comfort zone where your performance is most predictable. You end up recreating the same experiences from the same beliefs and behaviors, again and again.

In this moment, I want you to challenge what is good enough for you. I want you to imagine how different your life would be if all your "good enoughs" were actually visible for you to see. Now what if you could "turn up the thermostat" on every one of them?

When you turn up your thermostat, the heating system kicks in to raise the room temperature to match your new thermostat setting. Metaphorically, too many people ignore the thermostat and adapt to the temperature by either putting on a lot of clothes to warm up or opening the windows to cool themselves down. Putting on clothes or opening windows are temporary fixes that don't last. Instead, we should be turning the dial of the thermostat to raise us to a higher level of being.

> *You are not a victim of circumstances. You have the power to influence and control your circumstances.*

You are not a victim of circumstances. You have the power to influence and control your circumstances.

You are a thermostat, not a thermometer. A thermometer can report the temperature but not influence it. That's what a thermostat is for.

If you don't like the temperature in any area of your life, regardless of how hot or cold it is, you have the power to change the setting that controls it.

Stretch your comfort zone by bombarding your subconscious mind with new thoughts and images while "seeing" your goals as if they're already achieved.

To do this, you will need to raise up who you believe you are and focus on past wins. You also may need to rethink what you are capable of and clarify what you deserve. As you reflect on these three things and change or develop your answers, this will allow you to change your thermostat set point and comfort zone.

Where is your current thermostat set point? Where would you like it to be?

As the next illustration reveals, your self-image can climb. What ruts are you currently stuck in? Start redefining your self-image by challenging who you are, what you are capable of, and what you deserve. Overcome your current performance rut by changing the temperature of your thermostat and challenging your self-image.

Until you believe you deserve it, you won't get it. Stop living *beneath your privilege!*

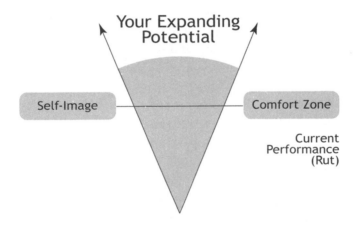

When you raise your self-image, it naturally creates a comfort zone above your current performance. The tension pulls you up from "performance ruts."

Repetition, Repetition, Repetition

There once was a time in your life when your subconscious mind was completely wide open. Because you were young and childlike, everything was fascinating. Your mind wasn't filtering much information yet, so you were taking it all in. Over time, the "watch guard" at the front of your mind began to take shape. The watch guard thought,

Hmm, I'm hearing a whole lot of different messages, and none of them are very consistent. Which ones have I heard the most?

That is how your subconscious mind works. It looks for the messages that it keeps hearing over and over and over and turns them into beliefs. Even if every once in a while, it hears information that contradicts this formed belief, it ignores it. It has established the "truth" and it is sticking to it, until you *bombard* it with different thoughts.

I know that using repetition sounds simplistic, but it really works. This same philosophy is successful with sports teams. One of the reasons the San Antonio Spurs and New England Patriots have dominated their sports for so long is that they keep hearing the same messages over and over on the fundamentals. How do you improve on the fundamentals? You do them over and over and over again.

In general, to move from where you are to where you want to go requires the same message to be repeated over and over. Once your creative subconscious mind buys into it, time collapses, and you simply begin to act like the new you. Your creative subconscious mind guarantees that your external experiences begin to match your internal belief system. This is self-image psychology in a nutshell.

> *In general, to move from where you are to where you want to go requires the same message to be repeated over and over.*

Engage your creative subconscious mind through affirmation and repetition.

Affirm, repeat.

Affirm, repeat.

Affirm, repeat.

I love seeing self-image psychology play out in everyday situations. The other day, I was playing golf with a friend who typically shoots a score around 100 over eighteen holes, but that day he played the front nine in 44 strokes. When he finished the front nine holes, he turned to me and said, "This is the greatest round I have ever had. I have never broken 90 before in my life when playing eighteen holes. If the back nine goes well, I may score 88!"

What do you think happened on the next nine holes?

You guessed it, he returned to his normal level of play. For the next nine holes, he shot a 56 to finish at 100. What is even more incredible is that he scored a par on the eighteenth hole to finish at 100.

On the front nine, even though he was playing great and had the potential to score well, his self-image as a golfer is set at 100 when playing eighteen holes. Because he was performing outside his comfort zone, he experienced tension and anxiety and found a way back to his comfort zone.

This also works in reverse. I am a pretty good golfer, and I typically score in the low to mid-80s over 18 holes. During the best round I have ever played, I finished with an 82. On the front nine holes, I had shot a 48, but on the back nine I shot a 34 to finish with an 82.

To get back to our "normal," it is amazing how the mind will cause us to either perform at amazing levels or sabotage our performance.

This applies to every area of your life. This principle affects your weight, your finances, and your job.

There are so many people who are in jobs that are far beneath their capability but consistent with their comfort zone. An example of this is commissioned salespeople who are comfortable earning a certain income. Remember, being comfortable does not mean they are happy with it; it just means they are used to it.

There are so many people who are in jobs that are far beneath their capability but consistent with their comfort zone.

What happens when they make their monthly quota early in the month? They relax, take it easy, and get some administrative work done.

What happens when they are short of the quota and it is close to the end of the month? They find a way to make it happen. They get creative and are filled with energy to get back up to where they are most comfortable.

This same principle also applies to relationships. I have a female relative who often says, "I don't know why I continue to find guys who don't treat me right." I shared with her this principle and explained that how she sees herself mirrors how others see her. I advised her that she must decide what is good enough.

Finally, a great young man entered her life. He treated her like a queen, honored and respected her. Everything she said she wanted in a relationship, he delivered. What do you think happened next? She broke up with him. She told me, "He is nice, but just not the guy for me."

The way he was treating her was outside of her comfort zone. She was used to guys who ignored her half the time. The fact is you attract people that are in alignment with how you see yourself.

> *The good news is that your old comfort zones do not have to be tomorrow's comfort zones. When you change on the inside, everything else will follow.*

The next time I saw her she was back with the same type of a guy she had previously complained about. The only difference was that he had a different name. Same problem dressed up differently.

Again, any time we are outside of our comfort zone, we feel anxiety and tension and either get back to where we belong or recreate the conditions that existed before.

The good news is that your old comfort zones *do not* have to be tomorrow's comfort zones. When you change on the inside, everything else will follow.

REFLECTIONS

- How you see yourself controls your attitudes, abilities, income, patience, etc.

- Your self-image is a complex picture of who you *believe* you are, what you *believe* you are capable of, and what you *believe* you deserve.

- When you attempt to perform outside of your comfort zone, you get anxiety and tension feedback urging you to "get back to where you belong."

- Your comfort zone is the range of performance where you feel most comfortable. It corresponds with your current self-image.

- Restrictive (fear) motivation is negative, extrinsic, and temporary. We get used to it or get away from it.

- Incentive motivation is positive, extrinsic, and temporary. It usually needs to keep getting bigger in order to keep working.

- Attitude motivation is positive, intrinsic, and long-lasting. Love of the activity is fundamental.

- It is important that you don't lower your standards or your goal. Raise the goal, and then raise your self-image to match it.

SELF-DISCOVERY QUESTIONS

1. What are some comfort zones in your life that you would like to change?

2. Where have you attempted to stretch beyond your comfort zone and felt tension and/or anxiety?

3. How do you motivate yourself?

4. How do you motivate others?

5. How do others try to motivate you?

6. What types of motivation do you use in your organization? In your family?

7. What kinds of motivation will you use in the future?

BUILDING SELF-ESTEEM

You May Change the World

Every day, a little old lady sits on a park bench in New York City and feeds the birds. On a particular day, she was feeling down, isolated, and discontented with life. A young man approached her. Pointing at the park bench, he asked, "May I have permission to take a seat?"

A bit surprised, she replied, "Why, of course."

The young man took a seat right next to her. "Do you mind if I feed the birds with you?" he asked.

"Why, no," she responded and handed him some bread.

They talked briefly as they both fed the birds. When he finished, he stood up and said, "Thank you for adding value to my day. I appreciate it."

As the young man walked away, the isolation and discouragement the old lady was feeling melted away. His small act of kindness restored her hope in humanity and herself. By adding value to his day, the value that she felt for herself went up as well.

Dr. Seuss advised, "To the world you may be just one person, but to one person you may be the world."

There are over seven billion people alive on earth today. It is easy to lose yourself in the crowd and feel insignificant and unimportant, but as Dr. Seuss advised, "To the world you may be just one person, but to one person you may be the world."

It is imperative that you recognize the worth and value that you contribute. Your thoughts, actions, and habits affect everyone around you and have the potential of changing the world.

More Than What You Do

Before I got cut from the Green Bay Packers, I remember walking into Lambeau Field in Green Bay, Wisconsin, where some of the best play-ers of all time were my teammates—the late Reggie White, Brett Favre, and others. I walked by fans and signed autographs as I entered our locker room.

Shortly thereafter, while sitting at my locker, a staff member told me that our general manager, Ron Wolf, wanted to see me. (Today, Ron Wolf is a member of the Pro Football Hall of Fame and is credited with being the orchestrator behind the resurgence of the Green Bay Packers's success.)

I was fairly nervous that Ron wanted to see me, so I jokingly responded, "Am I getting a new contract extension already?"

The staff member responded, "Be sure to bring your playbook with you."

Oh no! "Bring your playbook" was the equivalent to a police officer hearing, "Turn in your badge and your gun." My worst fear had come to pass. I was being released, fired and perhaps put nicely, promoted to fan. Ron Wolf said to me, "You have million-dollar talent and a lot of potential, but your body must hold up in order for that potential to become performance."

Ron proceeded to tell me the conditions of my release. I shook his hand and thanked him for the opportunity. He wished me well, and I cleaned out my locker.

After that moment, his words echoed in my head, and my greatest struggle was in my mind. I had to explain to friends and family why I was back home. I revisited this memory every Sunday when I watched peers of mine playing in the NFL. *Why am I here? Who am I now?*

The people who were impressed that I had made it to the NFL were no longer impressed. Those who celebrated with me when I was drafted were nowhere to be found. In my mind, I did not just fail—I was a failure. The narrative of my life had changed, and it took my self-image, self-esteem, and identity with it.

One of the challenges with self-esteem is that we are too identity-oriented versus action-oriented. Instead of evaluating our actions, too often everything translates to identity. Being a professional athlete was my identity, so when I lost my job, I also lost my identity. As my mentor, Bob Moawad, would often say, "If you are what you do, then when you don't... you aren't!"

Bob Moawad, would often say, "If you are what you do, then when you don't... you aren't!"

Your identity doesn't need to be challenged when you change your role in life. You are more than your job description; you are more than what you do.

At Lambeau Field, I had a glorious entry and a painful exit. One of the hardest parts wasn't that I was cut or that later I had to work as a janitor at night, but rather it was coming home and being limited to what my family could afford. That reaffirmed my failure.

When my oldest daughter, Taylor, was born, I had to set up a payment plan to pay for the doctor and hospital bill. Again, that reaffirmed my failure. I couldn't make the car payment or fix anything that broke. *Failure.* I couldn't afford car insurance either, another reminder that I had failed.

I could go on and on, but the point is, I was constantly reliving the failure experience, which reinforced it. I ruminated being cut from the NFL and relived that feeling of failure repeatedly in my mind and in my experience. My rumination fed my subconscious mind with real and imagined experiences of failure. I can't tell you how many times I replayed in my mind being cut, walking out, and feeling like a failure.

You are more than your job description; you are more than what you do.

I was experiencing "depression descent." I assumed that because I failed at football, I was going to fail at everything else. I placed a period where God placed a comma. My story was not over, yet I was living like it was. Not only was my life being affected by my poor mindset, but every relationship in my life was negatively affected as well.

> *People who do not accept themselves as valuable or worthwhile, tend to manifest their frustrations and insecurities in their interactions with other people.*
> —Dr. Walter Staples

What Is Self-Esteem?

Self-esteem is not egotism, conceit, or arrogance. It is not an intellectual inventory of all your favorable characteristics and assets.

Self-esteem is the degree to which you love and accept yourself as you are—the degree that you respect yourself and feel confident to deal with life's challenges.

It is how warm, friendly, and appreciative you feel toward yourself. It is recognizing that you are no more or less worthy than anyone else.

Jesus Christ said, "Love others as you love yourself." To properly love others, you must properly love yourself first. In order to care about other people, you must first care about yourself. The source of love for others is love for yourself. For me, the source of love for myself is God's love for me. I do not need to generate it; I just need to reflect it.

The Cauldron Theory, which captures the essence of this condition, states that in order to pour water into another person's cup, you must have water in your own. You can't give away what you don't have.

We all benefit when we feel better about ourselves. Zig Ziglar also identified this concept as one of the greatest success principles. He said, "If you help enough people accomplish their goals, you will accomplish all of yours. What you do for others, God will do for you when you truly decide to make that your life."

I was asked by a leader, "How can I get my people to respect me more?"

I responded with, "You are asking the wrong question. The question you should be asking is, 'How can I get my people to respect themselves more?'"

As a leader, how can you get the people around you to appreciate and respect themselves more? What would happen if people on your team had a one-notch rise in their self-esteem? Just imagine the possibilities!

Hostility: Indicator of Low Self-Esteem (Personal and Organizational)

Before we cover the Steps for Building Healthy Self-Esteem, let's discuss hostility and explore its framework.

Hostility is one of the indicators of low self- and organizational esteem.

For children, hostility reveals itself as pushing, shoving, or hitting another child when things do not go our way.

As adults, we become much more sophisticated with our temper tantrums and manifest hostility in three different ways:

1. Withholding
2. Attacking on the subconscious level
3. Having a fear of rejection (opinion of others)

Withholding

After leaving the NFL, my self-esteem took a nosedive and I became *hostile*. I began to withhold from others. I withheld my participation, praise, speech, information, and my best efforts. I stopped taking risks. I emotionally and mentally shut down and closed myself off from the world around me.

When you feel good about yourself, it is not necessary for you to withhold from others. It is easy to distinguish an environment where high self-esteem flourishes. People who feel good about themselves are much more productive, participate in healthy conversations, and share ideas where honest feedback is given and received.

When you are on a team with high self-esteem, you feel a sense of abundance. You want to *share* because there is plenty to go around.

Low self-esteem shrinks your perspective and you obsess about limitation and scarcity. When an NFL team picked up one of my good friends, instead of being happy for him, I thought, *That was one of the teams that was going to pick me up!* I felt like he took my one and only opportunity. Crazy, right?

Along those same lines, low self-esteem makes it hard to celebrate the success of another. If they make money, *they must be robbing someone. Cheating them blind! They are probably doing something wrong or sleeping with the boss.* The belief is that someone else's blessings limit what could come your way. Because of low self-esteem, we begin to live in a world of scarcity where money, opportunities, and possibilities are limited. As a result, we hoard what we should be sharing. We ridicule what we should be praising.

Love shares.

Attacking on the Subconscious Level

Another way to demonstrate hostility is to attack on the subconscious level, which is done with hurtful teasing and sarcasm. Others might be laughing on the outside, but the subconscious mind may be buying into what is being said.

Beware of attacks on the subconscious level.

When we use sarcasm or put-down humor, remember that "the axe forgets, but the tree remembers." The person telling the joke may forget, but those receiving the joke remember.

> *The axe forgets, but the tree remembers.*

We have hurt people, cut people, and destroyed hopes and dreams in the guise of humor—just to get a few laughs. The more you hear something, regardless of whether it is said sarcastically or not, the more you grow to believe it, especially when the words come from people with authority.

This is why growing your esteem level is so important. It strengthens your psychological immune system to handle the comments, eye rolls, and put-downs of others.

> *No one can make you feel inferior without your consent.*
> *No one can give you a compliment except yourself.*
> *Get in the habit of esteeming yourself.*
> —Eleanor Roosevelt

Fear of Rejection (Opinions of Others)

Having an unhealthy fear of rejection and opinions of others is an-other indicator of low self-esteem. Perhaps you are trying to be a mind reader, and you spend all your time wondering about what other people think about you. What a waste of time!

The fear of rejection holds your attention hostage as you focus on the opinions of others. And such fear attacks your self-esteem.

As I began my career as a public speaker, I *had* to grow my esteem level. It is difficult to be a public speaker and have low self-esteem. Your eyes immediately find the person with their arms folded, and you believe their body language is telling you, "Not only do I not want to be here, but I am actually getting dumber listening to you talk!"

When I'm speaking, instead of focusing on why that person has their arms folded, I focus on the impact my message will have on the entire audience. I think about what makes my message powerful and how each person will leave better than they came. As a result, feelings of confidence replace feelings of fear. Remember, feelings follow focus.

At age 18, you worry about what everyone thinks of you. At age 40, you stop caring what people think about you and at age 60, you finally discover that they weren't even thinking about you in the first place.

A problem for many people is the opinion they have of themselves is based primarily on the opinions others have of them. This is where the adage, "I am not who I think I am; I am who I think you think I am," rings true. When I look back over my life, I wasted far too much time worrying about what others thought of me.

Jack Canfield, author of *The Success Principles*, called it the 18/40/60 rule. At age 18, you worry about what everyone thinks of you. At age 40, you stop caring what people think about you and at age 60, you finally discover that they weren't even thinking about you in the first place.

My grandmother would often say, "Baby, ain't nobody thinking about you. Guess who they are thinking about…themselves. Stop wasting time worrying about others who aren't worrying about you." Thank God for grandmas!

Now you might be thinking, *Well, it's selfish to not consider what others are thinking*, but the fact is your fear of rejection is what is selfish. It is extremely selfish, because you are completely consumed with thinking about how *you* are being viewed.

High self-esteem is not that you think higher of yourself than others, and humility isn't thinking less of yourself. Humility is thinking about yourself ***less often***.

You can be concerned for other people, but don't obsess about what they are thinking about and how it relates to you.

In any endeavor, it is important to lock onto the positive. More importantly, healthy self-esteem prevents you from attempting to be a mind reader, being overly concerned about what others are thinking about you.

> *Stop wasting time worrying about others who aren't worrying about you.*

You can have a good self-image, but without healthy self-esteem, you will never bridge the gap between who you are now and who you want to become.

You cannot be a failure without your consent.

Healthy self-esteem helps you combat the voice in your head that's saying, "I am unworthy. I don't deserve to be great. This is too good for me. I am not…"

Low self-esteem is like having very few resources in your emotional bank account. Each time you go in to withdraw strength or confidence, you get an insufficient funds notice. When you swipe your self-esteem debit card, it's denied every time!

Heidi, an executive of one of my clients, traveled a lot because of her job. One day, she was in Southern California and decided to stop by a quaint souvenir shop that caught her eye. A friendly, elderly woman greeted her: "Can I help you find anything?"

"No, I am just browsing. I am from out of town, so I thought I would stop in really quick," Heidi replied.

"Oh, where are you from?"

"Boston."

"Wow, I have never been to Boston."

The lady, who Heidi learned was named Isabella, talked for over thirty minutes. Isabella had never been outside her local area, so she was intrigued with how many places Heidi had been.

"What is your address?" Heidi asked. During their conversation, Heidi had grown fond of Isabella and wanted to stay in touch. "Because I have the opportunity to travel so much with my job, I want to mail you a postcard from each city that I visit."

"I would love that," Isabella said with a smile.

For the next few years, Heidi sent postcards from each city she visited, and Isabella always wrote back. There came a period of time, though, when Heidi stopped getting letters back from Isabella. She kept sending postcards, but there was no response. Without having another means to reach her, Heidi patiently waited.

A few months went by and Heidi finally got a letter. It was from Isabella's daughter, who informed Heidi that Isabella had passed away. As the family was going through Isabella's belongings, they had come across a box full of Heidi's postcards. Recognizing the value of their relationship, Isabella's daughter reached out to Heidi and wrote her a long thank you letter. She thanked Heidi for allowing Isabella to see the world through Heidi's eyes.

> *To the world you may be just one person, but to one person you may be the world.*
> —Dr. Seuss

You Are a Human Becoming

The challenge with improving self-esteem is that who and what was around you in your earlier years heavily influence it. As an adult, it is much harder to change your self-esteem, because everything is either validating what you already believe about yourself, or you are rejecting the things that don't agree with what you believe to be true. This takes energy.

When those who should help shape your identity aren't there when you are growing up, you find their substitutes from other sources or, perhaps, not at all. You might confuse the opinions of others with your identity—you are not *who you think* you are, but rather who you think they think you are.

How serious is your identity problem? It's a bad thing to not know who you are, but it is even worse to be told who you are by people who don't really know who they are. Having low self-esteem is not virtuous.

> *You must realize that life is a process, a journey. If someone evaluates you early on, their feedback might be accurate, but it isn't complete or permanent.*

You have to be intentional and allow accurate information to reshape your identity. You must make the intentional decision that you want to improve this aspect of your life. If you don't, you will continue only to pay attention to the information that confirms what is already there.

Every day you can be honest about your strengths and weaknesses and remind yourself that you are doing the best you can.

A mentor of mine, Bob Moawad, would often say, "You are not a human being—you are a human *becoming!*"

You must realize that life is a process, a journey. If someone evaluates you early on, their feedback might be accurate, but it isn't complete or permanent.

Who are you becoming?

Seven Steps for Building Healthy Self-Esteem

There are seven steps for building healthy and strong self-esteem.

Your first step is to recognize that you are special and unique just the way you are.

There is no one else in the world like you. Just because there are billions of people on our planet, it doesn't mean you should devalue your uniqueness. Again, *there is no other person like you!* Do you realize what a miracle you are? As the Bible states, "You are wonderfully and fearfully made." The choices you make every day affirm your uniqueness.

One of my high school teachers, Rosa Cartledge, made me feel valued and special. She encouraged me and was genuinely happy to see me each day I walked into her classroom. High school was a struggle for me, but Mrs. Cartledge's words and smiles helped me understand that I was valued. She gave me the confidence to make things happen with my own initiative. She asked questions that allowed me to think for myself and encouraged me to value my own opinion as much as the opinion of others when I made decisions.

Speak the truth to yourself: *I am valuable and unique just the way I am.*

Who has impacted and influenced your self-esteem in a positive way?

Only Compete with Your Best Self

The second step in building your self-esteem is to reject the idea that you are in competition with others.

You are only in competition with your own *best* self. From a purely self-esteem perspective, there is no reason to compete with others. When you compete with yourself, your goal isn't to be the best; your goal is to *be at your best more of the time.* This mindset is for your benefit, because it helps you perform at your best. It is completely independent of what may be going on around you at school or at work. When you know you have given your best, you feel good about yourself in spite of the outcome.

There is always going to be a scoreboard, a competitor, or a team you are competing against, but by competing with your own best self, you raise the probability that the scoreboard works in your favor more of the time. You discover what your best is when you are in a healthy competitive environment rather than comparing yourself to others. Not only does the comparison game cause problems, but it also limits your perspective simply because your competition might not be all that good.

> *You are only in competition with your own best self.*

It is more than about winning; it is about discovering what is possible. We have so much potential that needs to be unleashed, and it is only unleashed when we commit to being at *our* best versus being *the* best. You may be the best on the scoreboard and still not be *at your best.* This is what makes healthy competition a good thing and unhealthy competition (just beating your opponent) a bad thing.

The Latin word for "competition" is *competere*, meaning "to strive with," not "to strive against." This is why every leader I coach and organization I consult, as well as sports teams (professional and amateur), win by making the primary goal to become their personal best.

As a leader, guide people away from believing they "have to" stack up to others. The comparison game has caused more unhappiness than we could ever imagine.

Personally, I strive to be the best husband, father, son, friend, leader, and human being that I can be. Who cares if I am a better husband than my friends are to their wives? I am not married to their wives—I am married to Cindy.

You are only in competition with your best self. When this becomes your mindset, neither wins nor losses define you. On the contrary, improving yourself does.

When you compete with your best self, your goal is to be at your best more of the time.

I am in competition only with my own best self.

Your Self-Worth Is Innate

The third step for building healthy and strong self-esteem is to recognize that your self-worth is innate.

> Your self-worth has nothing to do with your net worth, and it is independent of your actions and decisions.

Your self-worth has nothing to do with your net worth, and it is independent of your actions and decisions. We have the tendency to link our previous actions and decisions, especially our bad ones, to our self-worth. As you reflect on some of your prior actions and decisions, if you knew then what you know now, would you have done anything differently? Most of us answer "yes," because our actions and decisions are only as wise as the information they are based on.

Failure is not final. You learned your lesson and have better information now. Forgive yourself and move on. Forgive others and move on.

Forgive! Forgiveness is for you…for you!

Mike Murdock states that forgiveness is not the removal of information; it is the removal of the pain from it.

Allow forgiveness to transform you. Being angry or resentful shrinks your self-esteem, while forgiveness allows you to grow and move beyond the past.

Help people to recognize that they are more than their actions and decisions and that failing in a relationship, task, or job, does not mean they are a failure. Losing the game doesn't mean they are a loser.

My worth is innate and not heightened or lowered by my actions and decisions.

Accept 100 Percent Accountability

The fourth step in building self-esteem is accepting 100 percent accountability for your actions and decisions.

Notice that I didn't write 90 percent or 85 percent. You read it right—*100 percent.*

Healthy self-esteem and personal accountability go hand in hand. You are responsible for your great actions and decisions. Focus on your wins and celebrate your successes because they are a testament to your effort and good decision-making. On the flip side, you are also responsible and accountable for your not-so-good actions and decisions, but that doesn't mean that you should beat yourself up.

There is no one to blame or take credit for your actions and decisions other than you.

Responsibility moves your self-esteem up while blame moves your self-esteem down.

Here are a few steps that you, as a leader, can utilize to help your team become more responsible in decisions that impact them:

- Provide them with alternatives/options—when people know they have a choice, they are far more engaged. People are usually up on what they are in on.

- Allow them to recognize the benefits and consequences to each— instead of telling them, allow them to determine what is in it for them.

- Allow them to make the decision—this is the most critical part for you to allow. Healthy-esteemed environments are where decisions are made, not just problems being discussed. The more people feel empowered to make decisions, the more they are engaged in the organization's success.

- Hold them accountable—the benefit here is you are holding people accountable for what they decided to do versus what you decided for them. People are much more committed to accomplishing *their* goals than they would be to yours.

I have used this simple four-step process with teams all over the world, and it has radically improved their productivity, chemistry, and creativity. Leaders have shared with me that many of their breakthrough ideas as well as process improvements have come by following this simple four-step process.

Mistakes Are Stepping Stones

The fifth step is to appreciate that mistakes are stepping stones to achievement.

Mistakes are a prerequisite for success. They enhance your awareness and allow you to learn and grow. The probability of you making a mistake is 100%. Remember, failing at a task, a relationship, or a job doesn't make you a failure. Just because you made a mistake doesn't mean *you* are a mistake. It is a stepping stone to improvement.

> *The probability of you making a mistake is 100%.*

Sometimes people make drastic, reactionary decisions because of a poor outcome. Because of a bad relationship, they choose to never have another one. *Huh?* They are willing to sacrifice the possibility of love because of one bad relationship. Why? One of the greatest joys in life is to love and be loved.

Why do we allow our mistakes or mishaps to be so permanent?

How do we use our mistakes as stepping stones instead of walls?

What if we shared our mistakes and failures with each other?

What if we learned and grew by listening to each other's challenges?

Each one of us is living proof that life goes on after a mistake or a failure. We can overcome and live through our missteps.

As a leader, sharing and acknowledging your mistakes increases your credibility with your team. I understand how it is easy to let the fear of rejection or low self-esteem get in the way of such transparency. Most leaders worry that if their team actually knew about their mistakes, they would lose respect. The opposite is actually true. The sooner you acknowledge your mistakes, the more respect you receive.

Are you ready to start sharing your mistakes with your team? All of us fall. The great ones simply get back up.

Mistakes enhance my awareness, allowing me the opportunity to grow and improve.

Embrace One Day at a Time

The sixth step for building healthy and strong self-esteem is to realize that life is a journey to be embraced one day at a time.

When you have healthy self-esteem, you plan for the future and set goals, but you pay attention and live in the now.

At one of my speaking engagements, I met a gentleman who experienced a powerful transformation during a significant adversity as he learned the importance of embracing life one day at a time. This man had previously lost his child to Sudden Infant Death Syndrome (SIDS), and a year later his wife passed away as well. Can you imagine how tough that would be? He was devastated.

From that point forward, he had a bitter attitude and a depressed demeanor. He was angry at God, angry at the world, and angry with himself. He didn't know what to do or how to process these events in his mind.

Then one day, he met another great woman and fell head over heels for her. Even though he was hesitant because of his previous losses, they got married and had a son. As you can imagine, he checked the child every night in fear that the same thing would happen again. At this point, his child was now four years old, and everything seemed to be going well.

Sadly, shortly thereafter, this couple found out their son had leukemia. His worst fear had come to pass! He and his wife had thought that the most difficult time was over, and then they found out their child was terminally ill.

We can only imagine the anger, frustration, and powerlessness. It is hard to even put into words.

For the next five years, his son was in and out of treatment. This man was living in a fog, trying to cope with it all.

After hearing his story, I asked him, "How did you mentally turn things around?"

"My son changed me. In my head, my son had already passed. I was already grieving, but he was still here. One day, he came home and asked me to play. I told him that I didn't feel like it. In response, my son screamed, 'Dad, I am the one dying, not *you!*'

"In that moment, the weight of everything finally hit me. I had spent the last five years preparing myself to lose my son instead of being here and living with him right now. Over the next two years, we did everything. We embraced and enjoyed every moment together."

> *"Over the next two years, we did everything. We embraced and enjoyed every moment together."*

Hearing his story was a life-changing moment for me, too. When he told me about the funeral, he described it as a celebration. He had embraced the principle of living in the moment and made the most of the limited time he had with his son.

When we think about something that already happened or imagine what could go sideways later on, we become sad, anxious, and depressed. This is not living in the moment.

Freedom is always about living in the moment. You experience real joy when you can be where you are right now.

Yes, it is important to set goals and know where you are going, but live in the now. Right now is the only place happiness can be found.

Praise and Gratitude Pays

The seventh step is to recognize that praise pays even when things aren't going well.

I enjoy catching myself and others in the act of doing things right! I call this good-finding versus fault-finding. I praise specific behavior and actions and avoid using vague terms. This builds self-esteem because it keeps your focus set in the right direction.

This is why I finish each day by writing down my wins. Before I go to sleep, I ask myself, "What were my wins of the day?" By the end of the week, I review my list and feel great about how many wins I experienced. There will always be disappointments, but I usually don't need help to remember those. It is the wins, both large and small, that I need to remember.

What can you do to feed and strengthen your self-esteem?

I finish each day with writing down my wins.

Another way that praise pays is through appreciation and gratitude. Gratitude is so powerful—one of the greatest secrets to success. When you thank the people around you, not only do they feel appreciated, but it motivates them to do more. Sometimes simple words like "thank you" or "I appreciate you" have such a significant impact. Everyone needs gratitude, and gratitude is a gift that you have in abundance. You just need to give it!

A grateful person always gets what they need, because people love sharing with a person who has a grateful attitude.

The quickest cure for ingratitude, though, is loss. You can't teach a person to be grateful by giving them more, but gratitude can be learned through loss. As Joni Mitchell sings, "Don't it always seem to go that you don't know what you've got 'til it's gone…" I don't want the experience of loss to be the price of learning gratitude.

I choose to be grateful for my wife, my daughters, my family, my career, my city, state, and country. I am grateful for them as I look to improve them.

Think of some things that you may not be feeling grateful for. Imagine if those things were taken away. How does this make you feel?

Affirmative Reminders for Building Self-Esteem

As you work through the seven steps of building healthy self-esteem, I want you to use these affirmative reminders, also known as "I am" statements, to engage your subconscious and creative subconscious minds and create stronger beliefs about yourself. Using affirmative reminders is a practical step to improve your self-esteem.

We will dive more deeply into affirmative reminders in Chapter Nine, so make a mental note of these now and come back to them when you are creating your list of daily affirmative reminders.

- *I am valuable and unique just the way I am.*
- *I am in competition only with my own best self.*
- *My worth is innate and not heightened or lowered by my actions and decisions.*
- *Losing the game doesn't make me a loser. Failing at a task, relationship, or job doesn't make me a failure.*
- *I enjoy making my own decisions and choices and accept 100 percent accountability.*
- *Mistakes enhance my awareness, allowing me the opportunity to grow and improve.*
- *I enjoy living each day, one day at a time in alignment with my values and goals.*
- *I enjoy giving myself and others plenty of praise for our efforts.*
- *Life is a journey to be embraced and enjoyed one day at a time.*
- *Yesterday is a cancelled check; tomorrow is a promissory note.*
- *Today is a gift. That is why we call it the present.*
- *I capture every moment worth celebrating.*
- *I enjoy catching my team members in the act of doing things right.*

Remember, self-image is how you see yourself in your head. Self-esteem is how you feel about yourself in your heart.

REFLECTIONS

- Healthy self-esteem is the degree to which you love and respect yourself unconditionally and feel confident to deal with life's challenges.

- Self-image is how you *see* yourself. It has more to do with your head, whereas self-esteem is how you *feel* about yourself in your heart.

- The Seven Steps for Building Self-Esteem

  - Recognize that you are special and unique just the way you are.
  - Reject the idea that you are in competition with others.
  - Recognize that self-worth is innate.
  - Accept 100 percent accountability for your actions and decisions.
  - Appreciate that mistakes are stepping stones to achievement.
  - Realize that life is a journey to be embraced one day at a time.
  - Recognize that praise pays—even when things aren't going well.

SELF-DISCOVERY QUESTIONS

1. What do you do to show your unconditional warm regard for yourself at all times?

2. What are some things you can do to build the esteem of those closest to you?

3. On a scale of 1–5, how would you rate your organizational esteem level? (1 being low, 5 being high)

4. As an organization, what do you do to esteem each other?

5. Is your tendency in your organization to look for negative performance and qualities in each other, or for the positive? How about in your family?

Third
Quarter

How Did I Get Here?

THE POWER OF GOAL-SETTING

Life without Goals

Why do so many of the greatest athletes in the world struggle to adjust to life after sports? The reason is that they don't have any post-athletic goals. By the age of thirty, the athletes had either accomplished or missed all of the goals they'd set for themselves. Many of the greatest professional athletes have ended up in tragic post-career circumstances, because when their careers ended, so did their goal-setting.

Unfortunately, this was also my experience and because of the prevalence of this problem, I am often asked to speak to various professional athletic associations.

For professional athletes, their greatest money-earning period is while they are in their twenties and thirties. For the general public, though, the greatest money-earning period is in their forties and fifties.

Imagine if you made the most money of your life while you were in your early twenties. Your greatest money-earning period would be while you have the least amount of maturity. Can you imagine the problems with that?

My ability to play football in my twenties literally defined my value. This was really problematic for me, because I didn't retire from football voluntarily. As you know, my professional career retired me. This same phenomenon doesn't only happen in sports, but in other high-profile careers as well.

> *Taking the time to determine and set your*
> *true goals can prevent a wasted lifetime.*
> —Mike Murdock

The gap between your goal and where you are right now shrinks with the energy that you bring to it. But once you accomplish your goal, the energy dissipates.

Instead of ever retiring from something, you need to retire to something.

As an example, life expectancy drastically declines once an individual retires. It's a dangerous thing to retire from something, because just like with professional athletes, often when your career ends, so does your goal-setting. Instead of ever retiring *from* something, you need to retire *to* something.

Goal-setting is about creating purpose. It is a lifestyle, not an event.

We are teleological beings, which means we are goal-seeking creatures. When you don't have a goal to move toward, you focus on what currently exists. You still move, but instead of moving forward, you go around in circles. As you go around and around, you create a deep rut for yourself. Your status quo is the result and as time goes on, it becomes very difficult to get out of it.

Has this ever happened to you—whether or not you have retired?

Many people don't set goals, because they don't know how they are going to accomplish them. It is important to understand that you won't know the "how" until you are clear about the "what" and the "why."

Values Drive Purpose

Prior to clarifying your goals, it is important that you identify and prioritize your top life values. Values are the standards of our actions and the attitudes of our hearts and minds that shape who we are, how we live, and how we treat other people. They are the key to motivation, self-determination, resolution of conflicts, and a lifestyle with meaning.

We are all aware of celebrities, athletes, politicians, even friends and family members who achieved incredible fame and fortune only to end up a wreck just a short time later. It is a dangerous thing when your talent takes you where your character can't keep you.

Your goals should align with your values. You do not want to get to the top of the ladder of success only to discover it was leaning against the wrong wall.

What are the things that matter most to you? Your answer to this question identifies your values, and your values drive the direction that your energy flows. Your values represent your real desires versus your impulsive wants.

As you think about your answer, make sure to be honest with yourself. Sometimes we identify values that are not really our true values, because we are worried about what people may think about the values we choose. So be true to yourself.

Here are just a few examples of values:

- Health
- Prosperity
- Family
- Relationships
- Mastery
- Integrity
- Spiritual Growth

- Belonging
- Teamwork
- Friendship
- Peace
- Personal Growth
- Expertise
- Community

- Competence
- Communication
- Fairness
- Recognition
- Achievement
- Honesty
- Play

Using this list—and adding other values to it—I want you to take these steps:

- List your top values in life in any order that comes to mind.

- Now, select your top *five* values from the list above and place them in order of priority.

Values are a way of being, but their expression is in what you do. An outside observer assessing your values will only be able to use your actions as part of their evaluation, not your intentions. When it comes to values, people listen to what you say but *believe* what they see.

Here are some great questions to ask yourself when evaluating how well your values and behaviors align:

- If someone observed your life for the past six months, how you spent your time and money, and how you related to others, what would that person say your top five values are?

- How close do you think their list would resemble your top five values?

> *If someone observed your life for the past six months, how you spent your time and money, and how you related to others, what would that person say your top five values are?*

The goal of this exercise is to help you make these values a new set point on your thermostat.

When I went through this exercise, my top five values, in order of priority, were: faith, family, friendship, fitness, and finances. I then sought out feedback to determine if there was a variance or gap between what I said my values were and how I lived out these values. I asked my wife, Cindy, my daughters, Taylor and Madison, my closest friends, and my business associates this question: "Based on your observations of me, what would you say are my top five values in order of priority?"

I was stunned when I heard their answers! They mentioned most of my same values, but in a totally different order. It was a Significant Learning Moment for me.

This is where the rubber meets the road. We can shout our values to the world, but the world can't hear us because our actions are so loud.

Commitment to Live

I will never forget a young man whom I met at one of my sessions. He was an Army recruiter, married with a three-year-old boy, who had been in the reserves before being called to serve in Afghanistan.

One day while deployed he was driving a Humvee on a dirt road when—*boom!*—the vehicle detonated a roadside bomb. Fortunately, the bomb was buried deep in the ground, so instead of the explosion blowing up the Humvee, the vehicle flipped over. This young man lost consciousness and suffered a severe concussion, along with minor cuts and bruising. More significantly, his life flashed before his eyes. That moment changed him forever.

Before he'd left for Afghanistan, he wasn't the best husband and father. When he was home, he wasn't really there. When his wife wanted to go out and do something fun, he would list a hundred reasons why they couldn't afford it or why he didn't want to go.

But after the bomb explosion and soon after he regained consciousness and made it back to safety at his base, he immediately called his wife. After telling her what had happened, he apologized profusely for all of the excuses that he'd given for not living, and then he asked his wife to put his son on the phone: "Son, I promise you that we are going to live. We are not going to wait to live," and this soldier meant it.

This young man began to write down, not only a bucket list for himself, but also everything that he wanted to experience with his family.

By the time he returned home from Afghanistan, his list had sixty items. What is amazing is that he and his wife and son completed almost 80 percent of the list within the next eighteen months! They went to concerts, events, and even traveled all around the world.

One thing that really stood out to me during our conversation was this comment: "My salary has not gone up at all. We haven't ended up with more money or time. That roadside bomb gave me my life. My time and what I do with it is up to me. If my wife and I want an exciting life, we had better have exciting things to live for. That is what happened."

The roadside bomb was a significant life event that changed his life. He reevaluated his priorities and clarified for himself what it meant to really live out his values.

The Cure to Unhappiness

The areas listed below make up what we call the Potential Wheel.

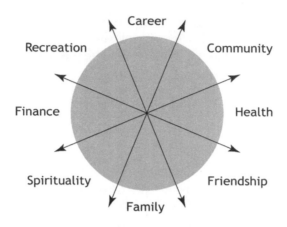

The Balance Wheel of Potential. The goal is to create a balanced and ever-expanding effectiveness that stretches out toward your full potential in every area.

The Potential Wheel encompasses eight areas of life that impact your overall happiness and sense of purpose. When you think about these various areas, are there any of them that feel stagnant in your life?

- Family
- Friendship
- Career
- Health
- Community
- Spirituality
- Finance
- Recreation

If some of these areas feel dormant to you, it's probably because you don't have any goals in that area. Am I right? Just like muscle in the body—if you don't set the right goals, these areas of your life will naturally atrophy, or waste away.

Earl Nightingale said, "The opposite of courage in our society is not cowardice, it is conformity." He also said, "The opposite of happiness is boredom."

You can't achieve happiness without goals. The cure to unhappiness is goals—exciting goals.

Show me a bored marriage, and I'll show you a marriage without goals.

Show me a person bored with their career, and I'll show you a person without career goals.

If you want an exciting life, you must have exciting goals to live for. The root is the goals; the fruit is the exciting life.

Your goals are the seeds. Don't be afraid to plant those seeds and begin to enjoy a more exciting life.

Just like muscle in the body, if you don't set the right goals, these areas of your life will naturally atrophy, or waste away.

Principles of Goal-Setting

These are seven principles for effective goal-setting that will help you design worthwhile and satisfying goals.

- **Balanced**
  - Create goals in all areas of your life. If you are feeling stagnant in one area, it might be because you are out of balance and lack goals in a particular area of your life.

- **Prioritized**
  - It is necessary to focus your attention in certain areas at certain seasons of your life. Your goals will look a bit different when your kids are in college than when they were infants and toddlers.

- **Positive**
  - State your goals positively with positive outcomes. Focus on what you want instead of what you want to avoid.

- **Clearly Defined**
  - Vague goals produce vague results. Define your goals with as much specificity as possible. Clarity helps focus. I encourage you to set specific deadlines for tangible goals. Avoid deadlines for intangible, attitudinal goals.

- **Exciting**
  - Lock onto an exciting, imaginable end result. Create your future *from* your future. Remember, you do not need to know how it is going to happen. Many people will not start until they know how, but the "how" will show up when you start. Go as far as you can see, and then you will see farther.

- **Keep Goals Confidential**
  - Share your goals only with active supporters. Share your goals with people who believe in you, who feed you with energy and who encourage you to never give up.

- **Update Goals Regularly**
  - Because life is a journey and not a destination, goal-setting must be a lifestyle, not a one-time event.

Disneyland

The principles of goal-setting work no matter how young or old you are. While facilitating the goal-setting portion of a MTG seminar for one of my clients, a participant leaped to her feet and said, "I have to tell the class about my granddaughter!"

Seeing her excitement, I responded, "Please tell us about her." With tears welling up in her eyes, she shared her story.

Her granddaughter loved everything Disney. She would watch Disney cartoons over and over again. At the age of seven, this little girl made a goal to get to Disneyland. She told her mother repeatedly, "Mom, I want to go to Disneyland. I want to go to Disneyland."

Her mother, with no fault of her own, kept telling her, "Baby girl, Mommy can't afford it."

The little girl got tired of hearing that, so finally she got mad one day and yelled, "Fine! I'll take us! You, me, and Grandma!"

Her mother would take the girl with her to work every Tuesday and Thursday, and this little girl noticed that there were no snacks available for the employees. "Mom, there's no snacks. Where can I get some? The employees need to have snacks!"

The next time they were at Costco, the little girl brought her piggy bank and bought a package of fifty small bags of potato chips. "Mom, your friends need some snacks." She was ready to start her business.

When her mother took her to work that next Tuesday, her daughter began selling her bags of potato chips for twenty-five cents each. Every employee bought a bag! This little girl quickly realized that she was on to something and wasn't charging enough. (Future business tycoon.) She raised her price and sold chips and other snacks every Tuesday and Thursday for the next year.

Lo and behold, she made enough money to take herself, her mother, and grandmother to Disneyland! Her grandmother worked for an airline company, so they were able to get their flights at a discount, along with a vacation package that allowed kids to fly free.

As they checked in at the Disneyland Hotel, the desk staff found out that this little girl had brought her family to Disneyland and paid for the whole thing. "Yes, I saved enough money to bring myself and my family to Disneyland," she told the Disneyland employee. Unbeknownst to the family, a manager overheard the conversation about how the little girl had brought her family to Disneyland and was totally impressed.

Come back and see us when you are eighteen years old. You are exactly what we are looking for—one who knows how to make her dreams come true.

When the family returned to their hotel room that night, there was a Disney princess dress on the bed with a note that read, "Come back and see us when you are eighteen years old. You are exactly what we are looking for—one who knows how to make her dreams come true." The Disney staff had also placed a job application next to the dress.

When the "why" is strong enough, even a child without resources can find a way to make things happen. As adults, we tend to have a library of excuses justifying why we won't go after a goal. This little girl shows us how to set aside excuses and get on to the goal!

Do you have a goal that you feel this strongly about?

Don't Worry about the "How"

Sometimes the "how" behind your goal can feel overwhelming, but it is important that you not concern yourself with the "how." You don't need to know the "how" before you start working toward your goal, because the "how" will show up when you start. Don't let your worry of the "how" paralyze you.

Abraham Lincoln acknowledged the importance of choosing your goal first when he said, "Determine the thing that can and shall be done, and then we shall find a way."

> *"Determine the thing that can and shall be done, and then we shall find a way."*

Begin by deciding what a better life looks like for you, whether it be career, income, home, spiritual life, relationships, community, or something else. Let yourself picture your ideals without worrying about how you are going to make them happen.

If you want to get from here to there, you must be clear about where *there* is. You don't know the price of the plane ticket until you know where you want to fly! Pick your destination first.

Set yourself free and decide what it is that you want and why you want it.

That is your responsibility! Eliminate the worry about the "how." If you focus on the "how" too soon, it will limit what you actually desire and want. You won't write down your exciting goals, because at the time you can't see "how" they can happen.

Don't set limits on yourself before you even get started!

In one of my sessions, a lady said, "Look, I am scared to write my goal down. It's like I am acknowledging that I really want this. I feel this anxiety about the fact that I'm actually writing it down."

I responded, "Yes, you're feeling anxiety. You are experiencing what happens when you acknowledge what your heart's desire is, what you're excited for, and it's outside your current comfort zone. You are feeling that healthy tension that kicks into gear when you set the thermostat at a higher level. Soon you will feel that energy kicking in to feel out how to close the gap between where you are and where you want to go."

Reasons come first; answers come second.

The Tip of the Football

As you contemplate your "why," the desire and energy to move forward becomes more powerful, yet the required action is still very simple. That is the goal.

Simple action, big meaning.

Being a former wide receiver, I now have the opportunity to coach many other wide receivers. This is a challenging position in football, because when you succeed, everyone sees it, but when you fail everyone also sees that. There is a ton of pressure behind catching or dropping the ball. It is simple—you either catch it or you drop it. There is no in-between.

When the ball is in the air, the players and the crowd hold their breath in anticipation. There is an adrenaline rush for everyone watching the ball, regardless of what team you are rooting for. Sometimes you can almost hear the anticipation in the air as people in the crowd stand up, hold their breath, and don't even blink as they await the outcome. *Just catch it!* What makes the moment so big is the amount of weight placed on a simple action.

While the ball is in the air, the wide receiver's brain analyzes all the associated stored information in mere seconds: *Have I caught the ball before? Have I dropped it? Did the crowd cheer when I caught it? Did my greatest fear come to pass because I dropped it?* Our amazing brain reviews fears, hopes, dreams, and desires, and all of it culminates in these few moments while the ball is in flight.

To lessen the weight of this moment for the players I coach, I instruct them to focus on only one thing: *Catch the tip of the football.*

When you are focusing so hard on the tip of the ball, all the other questions, information, and memories of failure can't get in. Your sole focus is catching that ball. You aren't worried about the times you dropped the ball in practice or previous games.

An additional tool that we use is the imagination. Not only can you focus on the tip of the ball, but you can repeatedly visualize catching the tip of the ball…over and over again. As a result, in the heat of the moment, your mind is more at ease because it has been here many times before.

People watching the game may ask, "How did you catch that?"

Your answer: "Exactly the way I have caught it a thousand times before in my mind." What gets pictured gets done.

Do you see how you can use this skill in your day-to-day life?

This ability to focus and visualize can be very effective when you are asked to speak in front of a group, solve a complex problem, or pass a test.

Maintain a laser-like focus on the task at hand and visualize your desired outcomes.

Keep Your Fire Hot

One of the principles of goal-setting is to keep your goals confidential and share your goals only with active supporters. If you share your goals too soon with people who don't believe in you or your goals, they can put out your fire.

You might hear responses like:

- Who do you think you are? No one in our family has ever done that!
- What makes you think you are so special?
- Doing that seems impossible!

Their criticism and fears can squelch your desire and confidence. Create a bonfire with your burning desire and belief in yourself. You want to keep your goal confidential until the fire is hot enough to be able to burn off any wet logs of criticism. Once your bonfire is strong enough, it can handle critiques, criticism, and the disbelief of others.

Until then, it is vulnerable. It is a little flame that constantly needs more kindling. It needs positive support and attention. And, unfortunately, every so often your flame will go out. Perhaps your goal or desire wasn't quite strong enough to weather the elements. Don't feel bad that you started something and couldn't keep it going.

When you are ready, create a flame again. Find people who will fuel your fire, as opposed to putting it out. Eventually, you will develop the skill to use people's criticism to make your fire hotter.

How many active flames do you have burning? Have you turned them into bonfires?

As a leader, it is important to provide positive support to the people around you and to keep their fires hot. Facilitate a culture of engagement, passion, and vision. Get them excited about the goal and how the outcome will improve their experience.

As Antoine de Saint-Exupéry wrote, "If you want to build a ship, don't herd people together to collect wood and don't assign them tasks and work, but rather teach them to long for the endless immensity of the sea."

> *Find people who will fuel your fire, as opposed to putting it out.*

People who "long for the immensity of the sea" find a way to build the ship. Establish the vision, then let the details follow.

Set *Through* Your Goals

Goal-setting is not an event—it is a lifestyle. Goals set new directions and broaden your perspective, so it is important to keep them updated.

As I have mentioned previously, when you attain a goal, energy is lost. You must create a new goal to maintain your momentum. For example, so many people create a goal for their wedding, but not for their marriage.

*The key is to set **through** your goals, not just to your goals.*

The goal isn't just to make it to the Superbowl; the goal is to win the Superbowl. Once you win it, the next goal is to win it again.

The late Earl Nightingale divided the world into two types of people: river people and goal people. Earl defined river people as individuals who "wade in the river" of their passion. Once they are involved in their passion, they don't need a goal to drive them. They get lost in what they are doing and don't even think. Many hours pass before they even look at their watch. They are completely consumed by what they are doing.

For example, Albert Einstein was consumed with discovery and curiosity. I believe Tiger Woods is another example of a river person.

For myself, I love to read leadership and self-help books. I don't need a goal to remind me to read. I am infatuated with learning. That is what drives me and keeps me interested.

So even though not all of us need a goal to get motivated, goals allow everyone to maintain balance in their lives. If one area of your life is totally consuming, by default you will neglect the other areas. If you update your goals regularly, it ensures that you will continue to be intentional in all areas of your life, not just with the ones you are passionate about. Be intentional about both the wedding and the marriage!

Can you think of any additional areas in your life where you could use some goals?

Define and Clarify Your Goals

When it comes to goal-setting, sometimes it is hard to even know where to start.

There are two types of goals—internal and external.

Internal goals are related to skills, hobbies, or personality traits. Perhaps you want to get better at making wise, effective business decisions or maybe you want to exercise effective leadership. Internal goals are difficult to measure, because they are more subjective in nature and a bit vague.

External goals have a specific outcome and are measurable. This is why you set a time limit on external goals, but not on internal ones. An example of an external goal would be increasing your income by $25,000 by the end of this year.

With internal goals, it is important to define what your desired outcome will look like. If one of your internal goals is to demonstrate more closeness and respect with your family, you need to decide up front the appearance of the outcome. It might be more one-on-one conversations with your spouse and kids or it might mean taking your kids to school every day. Either way, you need to clarify that for yourself so that you can hold yourself accountable.

As you think about possible external goals, ask yourself these questions to clarify your intent:

- Why am I doing this?
- Do I really want this goal?
- Will this help me achieve what is really important to me?
- Is this good for me, my family, and my business?

- Would I be fulfilled?
- Can I achieve more?

What external goals do you want to set in the various areas of your life, including family, friendship, career, health, community, spirituality, finance, or recreation? Do you want to take your family on a vacation? Do you want to lose ten pounds? The possibilities are endless and completely up to you to decide.

Goal-setting is designing the mental picture of what you want your life to look like before you experience it.

The mental picture that you design today becomes tomorrow's manifestation.

Give yourself the permission to think and dream big! Write down your goals— whatever comes to mind. Go as far as you can see in your mind. Over time, you will see even further.

Foresight, rather than hindsight, will get you where you want to go. It's the reason we have a really big windshield on our car and a really small rearview mirror. Look forward!

What excites you? What are some things that you really want to do, really want to be, or really want to have?

Tim Ferriss states, "Ninety-nine percent of people in the world are convinced they are incapable of achieving great things, so they aim for mediocre. Therefore, the level of competition is fiercest for realistic goals." (*The 4-Hour Workweek*)

> *"99 percent of people in the world are convinced they are incapable of achieving great things, so they aim for mediocre. Therefore, the level of competition is fiercest for realistic goals."*
> —The 4-Hour Workweek

At a minimum, come up with at least ten goals. Use the areas of the Potential Wheel that I referenced earlier in this chapter as a framework.

*Stop…*and complete the goal-setting activity now!

Think Beyond the Past

As you go through this process of writing down your goals, don't limit yourself by your past experiences or people that have always told you what you can and can't do. Many of us have experienced some type of bully in our lives. Perhaps at the playground they kept throwing rocks at you, saying, "You can't go over and play on my swings; you have to stay right here!"

If you are not careful, you will set goals based on the bully and this little playground where you used to play. You are on a much bigger playground now, and the bully is gone—although he or she may still exist in your mind.

This mind bully often manifests itself as a *"yeah, but"* voice in your head. The *"yeah, but"* voice isn't you! It's something said by someone else years ago that is still influencing you today. Regardless of the origin of the *"yeah, but"* voice in your head, you must conquer it and turn it into an ally. This *"yeah, but"* voice is stretching you, and soon that same voice will begin to encourage you versus discourage you.

How can this be? This voice is your creative subconscious mind at work. It is your job to make it work for you instead of against you. As you write down your goals, you can remove all these kinds of limitations in your mind.

Don't worry if your spouse or someone else disagrees or if even you think it is impossible!

There are so many methods to accomplish every goal that you have. I have already shown you that out of the four billion bits of information that hit your brain every second, only two thousand bits actually get through. Out of that two thousand, the majority of them are just regurgitated information that already existed. That means there are over three billion bits of information that aren't getting through to your conscious mind, because all of that is being filtered out by your limited thinking.

Do you really believe it's not possible to accomplish your goals? *Don't buy into it!* We work from such a small fraction of the information that is available to us that for you to conclude it is not possible for you to accomplish your goals is just a big lie. Stretch your thinking.

*Now, what goals do you **really** want to achieve? As you set goals, you gain the clarity that you need to move forward.*

You are familiar with my story. After being cut from the NFL, I was a night janitor cleaning US West buildings, but I wanted to be an international keynote speaker and consultant. My goal and purpose were to train, coach, and inspire leaders like yourself all over the world in unleashing their potential, as well as the potential of those around them. Keep in mind, I set this goal when I was cleaning buildings.

The only group that I could practice my "keynote speeches" on was the basketball team of eight-year-old boys that I coached. My pre-game and half-time speeches may have been the best in the world, but we still lost every single game! We probably should have been working on passing and dribbling, but I was speaking too much. But we sure had the inspiration down!

During the year and a half that followed, I was begging people to listen to me. But I had my goal in mind…and today the top companies in the world solicit my support, and I get to travel and speak to their executives and employees.

I am not sharing my story to impress you, but rather to *impress upon you* that these principles work. I am not teaching you based on what I have heard, but what I know and have experienced. I am an inspired practitioner of the MTG principles because they work!

Maybe you have a significant primary goal that you want to focus your energy on? My primary goal was speaking and consulting, but I had other goals too. Ultimately, many of them were enabled and achieved because I was very clear on my primary goal.

> *What is the one goal that would change everything for you? Make it big.*

Your primary goal is your game-changer, the one that will make all the difference.

What is the one goal that would change everything for you? *Make it big.* My ultimate goal is to inspire you to have a really big goal. The truth is that it is easier to obtain what you really want than to settle or compromise. I will show you how to grow into your goals, versus settling for a goal that fits where you are currently.

Become Constructively Motivated

Here are four practical steps to help you become even more motivated to accomplish your goals:

1. Visualize both the desired changes, as though they were already occurring, as well as the reasons why you want the changes to occur.
2. Gather the correct information and skills you need. Lock out negative and unnecessary distractions. Be confident that setbacks are merely temporary and provide you with feedback to improve.
3. Permit yourself learning mistakes. A mistake is simply another way to do something based on your awareness. There is no such thing as a straight line from where you are to where you want to be! Many times, goals work the same way. You will make learning mistakes on your journey and feel like you went backward or sideways. If things don't go as planned and the route looks a bit different, be open to it. A few steps backward gives you a running start forward.
4. Repeat your success over and over. This will eventually put the skill into your subconscious mind.

If you cannot see your goal in your mind, you will not see it in your future.

Constructively Motivate Others with Dignity

Here are six powerful principles to help you constructively motivate others with dignity to accomplish their goals:

1. Help them see the benefits. Answer the "why" questions. Take the time to explain the motivation behind your plans.
2. Relax the person to whom you are presenting the new information. Tension creates stress, and stress leads to a toxic environment.
3. Involve or fascinate them with this new information. Make the task exciting and fun. Be enthusiastic and help them visualize both the end result and the benefits.
4. Eliminate the use of restrictive phrases ("have to, can't, should, ought to, won't") and replace them with constructive phrases ("want to, can, decide to, going to, intend to, choose to").

5. Substitute constructive criticism for constructive direction. No one enjoys being criticized. Tell people a) what the task is, b) why it is important, and in some instances c) how to accomplish it. People are typically "up" on what they are "in" on.

6. Offer praise and recognition for a job well done.

   a. Praise all approximations moving closer to the desired result.

   b. Look for specific items to praise.

   c. Build up by default. (Don't "put down.")

   d. Remember to congratulate frequently for a job well done, no matter how small. You can't appreciate someone too much. Celebrate the success of others around you.

Become a Success Magnet

Now that you have defined your goals and what success looks like for you, it is important to realize what author Jim Rohn points out: "Success is not something you pursue, but success is attracted by the person you become." Now that you have your goals, don't chase them.

> *You can't appreciate someone too much. Celebrate the success of others around you.*

Your task isn't to go work hard on your goals. Your task is to work hard on you and to strengthen your belief in achieving the goal.

Your brain will align your outer world of experiences with your inner world of goals. The real challenge is to become congruent from the inside out, and that is what the next chapter is all about. There we will begin the process of getting your belief system congruent with your goals, instead of limiting yourself to goals that match your current self-image.

You are now ready to make your dreams and goals a reality. Let's go!

REFLECTIONS

- Goal-setting is designing what you want your future to look like.

- Goal-setting is a lifestyle. Instead of retiring *from* something, you need to retire *to* something. Goal-setting is about creating purpose.

- When you set goals, the real value comes from the "why."

- Principles of goal-setting:

  ○ Balanced
  ○ Prioritized
  ○ Positive
  ○ Clearly defined
  ○ Exciting
  ○ Confidential
  ○ Updated regularly

- The key is to set *through* your goals, not just *to* your goals.

- There are two types of goals—internal and external. Internal goals are related to skills, hobbies, or personality traits. External goals have a specific outcome and are measurable.

- Your primary goal is your game-changer. It is the goal that makes all the difference.

- Energy flows in the direction of your goals.

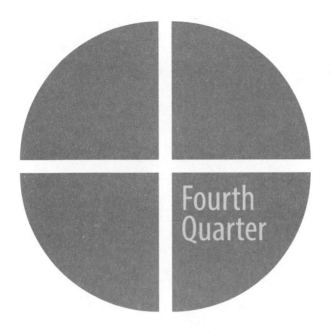

Fourth
Quarter

How Do I Get There?

9

BELIEVE IT, THEN SEE IT

Chilling with a Purpose

On this journey together of MTG, the time has come for you to *intentionally* tell your mind what it is that you actually want. What you have in your life now is an indicator of what you have been telling yourself. If you want to know what you have been saying in that internal conversation, simply look around. Your results are an indicator.

If you want something different, then you must tell your mind something different. You must keep telling your mind that you want… your goals!

Your external world of experiences will eventually match your internal world of goals.

High performers *dwell* on what they want to have happen, and they move toward it. On the other hand, low performers *dwell* on what they don't want to have happen and move toward it.

One day I was in my home office lying in my massage chair, and my daughters came in the room. "Daddy, what are you doing?" they asked.

"Baby, I'm just dwelling."

"Dad, what is dwelling?"

"It's chilling with a purpose."

I was focusing my mind on my goals. Visualizing all my goals as if they have already taken place. Research indicates that when we spend time thinking, visualizing, and dwelling on something, it is time very well spent. We need to get past the belief that such focused, thoughtful reflection is a waste of time.

It actually saves you time. It opens up your eyes so you can see the difference between activity and productivity. The truth is that visualization is more productive than any other activity you can do.

Remember, goal-setting is a conscious act. Goal attainment is a subconscious act.

> *Visualization is more productive than any other activity you can do.*

Dr. W. Edwards Deming, widely acknowledged as the father of the quality management movement, emphasized that when you get the first 10–15 percent of a project right through thoughtful preparation, it guarantees that 80–85 percent of the project will go well.

We tend to undervalue this meditative part of the process. We rush into action instead of being intentional.

To clarify, I am not advocating for you to overanalyze everything to the point where you don't move. I am advocating that you pay particular attention to the first 10–15 percent of planning, preparation, and effort. This includes visualizing the end state and imagining what the goal, task, or outcome will look and feel like when accomplished.

As a leader, spend some time "dwelling" daily. When someone asks you what you are doing, tell them you are "chilling with a purpose."

> *As a man thinketh in his heart, so is he.*
> —Proverbs

In the previous chapter, you defined and clarified your goals, as well as identified a major breakthrough goal. Now that you have identified the "there" that you really want, it is necessary to understand how your imagination and belief system play a significant part in reaching your goals and creating meaningful and lasting change in your life.

The focus now is on how you grow belief. As this chapter's title indicates, you will see it only *after* you first believe it.

It is time to learn how to rescript your thinking with the use of affirmative reminders and mentally experience the "you" you want to become. Affirmative reminders will allow you to discover and speak to the greatness in you.

Let's work together to challenge your current belief system and grow into who you were meant to be!

The Greatest Nation in the World

The greatest nation in the world is the Imagi-nation. It has no boundaries. It is never too late to engage the power of your imagination and become who you were meant to be.

As you think about your goals and dreams, it is important to ask yourself, "What kind of a person do I need to be to do the things I want to do and have what I want to have?"

Imagine what it would be like to be that person. Imagine what your beliefs, habits, and attitudes would be. Do you have a good visual of what the "new and improved you" would look like? Do you believe that this person *could* be you?

> *"What kind of a person do I need to be in order to do the things I want to do and have what I want to have?"*

> *Your imagination is a preview of life's coming attractions.*
> —Albert Einstein

This is why the word "belief" is so important. It is a common word that is used often, so we don't always grasp the power and significance of it, but it impacts everything. Belief is defined as a state or habit of mind in which trust or confidence is placed in some person or thing.

Your behaviors are simply beliefs acted upon.

My desire to be a better husband, father, leader, speaker, consultant, golfer, etc., is not enough. My behaviors are *influenced* by my beliefs. The same is true for you. If you want to change a behavior, you must change a belief.

The sermons and locker room speeches that have truly inspired me all have had a common theme—"believe." As we discussed in Chapter Four, your willpower will almost always come in second to your belief system. Instead of fighting a losing battle by only using willpower, use your belief system to create change.

Flood Your Mind

We improve our actions and decisions (behaviors) by replacing wrong information with right information, old beliefs with new beliefs, fear with confidence, and boredom with exciting goals.

How do we do this?

Imagine there is a pitcher of dirty water on the table and your task is to replace the dirty water with clean water, but you can't move or pick up the water pitcher. How would you do it? The only way is to *flood* the pitcher with clean water until the only water that remains is clean water. It is a simple process, but it may take a significant amount of clean water to displace the dirty water that was in there.

For many people, the process of change is daunting because they attempt to clean out the pitcher of dirty water one speck of dirt at a time.

When you flood your mind with the right information, your actions and decisions (behaviors) will improve.

Because you are flooding your mind with the right information, it isn't necessary to go back twenty years and deal with every single reason why your water is dirty in the first place. You simply need to start where you are right now to make significant changes in your life.

Flooding begins with changing your thoughts, as well as changing the images that lead to those thoughts. This begins the process of real change—altering *how you think*, because all behavior is simply a thought acted upon. When someone makes the statement, "You need to change the way you behave," what they are really saying is, "You need to change the way you think."

The root is the thought, and the fruit is the behavior or the result.

> *When you get the correct operating thoughts into*
> *your subconscious mind, you become what*
> *you are capable of becoming.*
> —Bob Moawad

The Self-Management Cycle

Are we controlled by our thoughts, or are we controlling our thoughts? The traditional cycle for change, illustrated below, shows how powerful our beliefs can be.

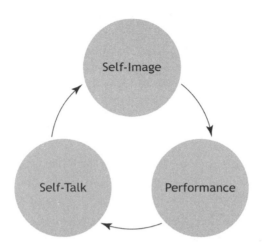

The Traditional Cycle for Change. Self-Talk influences Self-Image, which influences Performance, which influences Self-Talk.

The traditional cycle for change is a great illustration of how powerful belief can be. As you know, your beliefs, habits, and attitudes are stored in your subconscious mind. Your attitude is the habitual way of thinking that controls your spontaneous reactions, and your habitual beliefs govern your behavior.

The traditional cycle for change perpetuates your existing performance, which is great when you are performing well. When you perform well, you say encouraging words to yourself, your self-image and self-esteem rise, and others give you positive feedback.

When you perform inadequately, the exact opposite occurs. You criticize yourself, your self-image and self-esteem fall, and you receive negative feedback.

In the traditional cycle for change, it is easy to get stuck in an endless loop of reinforcing behavior that is hard to break, especially when your performance is poor. You give yourself negative feedback, which may be completely accurate, but it still lowers your self-image and self-esteem, which in turn leads to more poor performance. A really bad cycle. This illustrates why change is so hard.

Perhaps a brother or sister tells you that you are horrible at art at age seven. They say, "That is so ugly, you can't even color inside the lines!" You affirm your performance and tell yourself, "Oh, they are so right. My picture looks ridiculous." Your self-image and self-esteem falls. You are asked to draw another picture on another day. You observe your picture—it isn't much better than your first one. Again, you tell yourself that you are lousy at art. Your self-image of not being good at art has now been validated.

Unfortunately, this is how the traditional cycle can create long-lasting beliefs that shape and limit your life. To change, we must interrupt this cycle.

Imagine what happens when someone who has told themselves over and over, "I am not very good in front of people. I am a terrible public speaker," is asked to say something in front of a group. What is their self-talk like as they stand up? *Oh my, I have to speak? I know I am going to blow it! Is my fly down? Does my hair look weird? I can't speak in front of groups! I know I can't do this..."*

Words trigger pictures, so simultaneously this person is picturing a huge mess-up. She looks around the room in terror. This self-talk then cycles into the self-image and self-esteem, which are the performance regulators. The creative subconscious goes to work and makes sure that the performance matches what has been affirmed internally.

The mind then creates blind spots to block out any information that is contradictory to the internal beliefs. If there is a supportive person in the audience, the speaker doesn't see them. But if two people are whispering to each other, the speaker sees them and assumes they are making negative comments or even making fun.

Do you want to place a bet on what happens next? To no surprise, this person struggles through the speech, sits down and says internally, *See, I knew I was a terrible speaker.* And the cycle repeats over and over—a self-fulfilling prophecy.

The traditional cycle for change does not improve performance.

It simply reinforces the performance that currently exists, which is great when you are already performing well. It doesn't work in your best interest when there is an area you need to improve.

You must change your approach and stop using performance as the primary measurable for improvement.

Take Ownership

You don't need to accept life the way it comes at you. You can design life the way you want it to be. When life doesn't come to you the way you would like, you can choose positive ways to respond to it.

Magic starts to happen when you remove performance from the equation for a period of time and take personal responsibility and accountability for growing your own self-esteem and self-image. This is called the "responsibility cycle" or the "self-management cycle" for change, which is illustrated below.

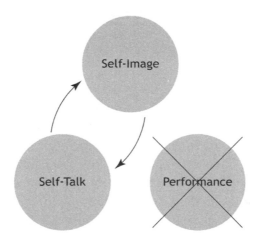

The Responsibility Cycle for Change. Self-Talk influences Self-Image, but you take responsibility to assure that bad performance doesn't influence Self-Talk or Self-Image.

This cycle provides the opportunity for you to take personal responsibility and accountability for your own inside image. You can improve your self-talk, which will improve your self-image and your self-esteem. As your performance regulators (self-image and self-esteem) improve, so will your performance. The self-management cycle eliminates negative feedback based on performance.

Now, I understand if removing performance from the equation makes you feel uncomfortable. Perhaps what I am telling you goes in the face of everything that you know and believe about performance. You might be thinking, *Eric, are you telling me that I am supposed to improve performance by ignoring performance?* Yes! You need to do this for a period of time while you allow yourself to grow your belief in yourself and your possibility.

*You won't be able to use **performance** as the criteria of how you coach yourself. You will have to use **potential**.*

This concept is no different than how we treat toddlers who are learning how to walk. We constantly encourage and praise them, even though they continually stand up and fall down. We don't say to them, "Quit falling! What is wrong with you?"

We have all been conditioned to believe that performance is the end-all and be-all, so even though this truth that I am advocating for is liberating in concept, it can be hard to embrace and accept. Just remember that your self-image doesn't need to be performance-dependent; it's a performance regulator.

To use the "responsibility cycle for change," you begin with your self-talk. This is the area you have the most control over and can influence immediately.

In Chapter Two, we talked about being born to win and conditioned to lose. Our conditioning often limits us, because it is weighed down with negativity and limiting beliefs. The responsibility cycle for change is also conditioning, but it is done *on purpose*. You are intentionally giving yourself new thoughts and beliefs that are in alignment with who you want to become.

When you are aware of how your mind, self-image, and self-esteem regulate your performance, you can use the self-management cycle to your advantage and give yourself the edge you need to accomplish your goals.

Using this cycle is especially effective when you go into a new role or must perform at a new level. Your focus will be on raising your image to a place where your performance has to match. You raise your expectations and beliefs and don't worry about your performance for the time being. You create change from the *inside out*.

Performance is the lagging indicator. Your self-talk is the leading indicator.

Constructive Self-Talk

As you focus on your self-talk, it is important to use objective, constructive feedback on yourself. As I discussed before, you must coach yourself *forward* and build yourself up. While you are ignoring your performance, you are going on an internal marketing campaign!

In the NFL, you don't wait until after you win the Super Bowl to get the team to believe they are champions. They have to see themselves as champions during the season, and the same is true for you. For this period of time that you commit to improving your self-talk, you must ignore your personal scoreboard.

As a leader, it doesn't mean that you and your team ignore your metrics and standards; rather it means that you focus your energy on giving objective and constructive feedback to the team. Remember, you are changing the root. The fruit will show up shortly thereafter, but not immediately.

Your self-talk, ability to visualize, and use of affirmative reminders are the tools that you will use to influence and improve your self-image and self-esteem.

As a leader, you can use this same process to improve your organizational image and esteem level. You will flood your team with the organization's vision, values, and goals, as well as create an environment that encourages personal development. By investing in the personal growth of your team, you create a culture that allows people to be at their best.

> *Your self-talk, ability to visualize, and use of affirmative reminders are the tools that you will use to influence and improve your self-image and self-esteem.*

In their book, *The Leadership Challenge*, James Kouzes and Barry Posner's research concludes that an organization's level of engagement is more of a result of individual employees being in tune with their own personal values and goals, not just the organization's.

Change expert Dr. John Kotter also confirms this, adding, "Any change effort that does not include opportunity for individual improvement and growth will fail."

When the values and goals do not engage employees emotionally, the change effort accomplishes very little. There might be a lot of activity, but not much progress. The natural laws governing effectiveness will win out.

To create long-lasting change, engage the hearts and minds of the people around you.

Roots of Change

Take a look at the illustration below. As a reminder, the "V" represents your potential in any area of your life. The left side represents your belief system within your subconscious mind. The right side of the "V" represents your willpower within your conscious mind. Your self-image is responsible for the vast majority of your behaviors, while your willpower is responsible for only a few behaviors here and there.

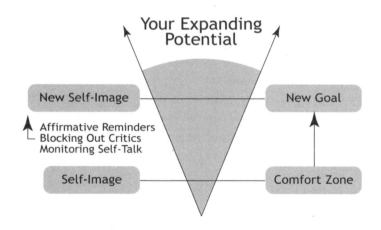

This "V" illustration measures your ever-expanding potential and effectiveness. The left side is where belief systems within your subconscious mind do their work. By creating affirmative reminders, blocking out critics, and monitoring self talk, you can raise the self-image, which naturally raises your comfort zone.

As you already know, this is not a fair fight. When you focus your energy on only the right-hand side and use your willpower to move from your comfort zone to your goal, your success rate will be small. An additional challenge is that even if you get close to your goal or even reach it, you can't sustain it because your self-image hasn't risen up to match your goal. The anxiety and tension that has been created will kick in and pull you right back down to where you are most comfortable.

You must create a new self-image that aligns with your goal.

There are three specific steps that you must take to elevate your self-image, steps that will lift you out of the comfort zone that you've created for yourself:

1. Monitor self-talk
2. Block out the critics
3. Imprint a new reality using affirmative reminders

Monitor Self-Talk

Words are tools that predict and perpetuate performance, so we need to monitor our words carefully. Self-talk is an integral part of the MTG process.

Words trigger pictures that bring about emotions. What you repeatedly hear and tell yourself, you will grow to believe.

Bombard your self-image and your self-esteem with positive self-talk to grow your belief.

As I focused on my goal to be a better husband, I told myself over and over, *I am a good husband. I am a caring husband. I treat my wife with significance.* Keep in mind that as I was saying this to myself, there was little evidence to support such statements. Everything on the inside of me was screaming, *Liar! Not true!* However, what I was doing for myself is no different than what a coach does for a team or a parent does for a child.

When a toddler takes her first steps, we celebrate it like crazy! We say, "Look at you, you are walking!" even though she only took one step and fell to the floor. We are affirming the toddler's potential, and we need to do the same thing for ourselves.

Coach yourself through an improved self-image, even though you might not have any supportive evidence.

If you don't do it for yourself and wait for someone else to come along and do it for you, you may be waiting for a very long time.

Block Out the Critics

Many people are more satisfied with the status quo versus things being different. This includes anyone who would rather talk about the past instead of discussing the future and who appears unhappy with any progress that you make.

You must knock out the criticism of others that reminds you or pulls you back to where you existed.

The challenge is that sometimes the critics in your life are the individuals who "love" you the most. It is difficult because deep down they really do want what is best for you, but the change disrupts the relationship dynamic.

In the movie *When a Man Loves a Woman*, Andy Garcia's character loves his wife to death. She is an alcoholic, and Andy's character has taken incredible care of her—but that became their comfort zone. When she quits drinking and gets healthy, it changes the dynamic in their relationship dramatically. What she needs from him now isn't the same as before, and he becomes very uncomfortable. This is common in a relationship when one of the individuals drastically changes.

Another challenge is that your critics could be the ones most affected by your poor performance. Using my goal to be a better husband as an example, I can't go to my wife and say, "If you want me to be better, I need you to be a better cheerleader for me." She's the one suffering from my deficiency as a husband and has plenty to say about my poor level of performance in this area. She is just telling me the truth. I should not expect a ringing endorsement from her!

For a while, I had to respond to her critiques by saying to myself, *I am a good husband. I am a caring husband. I treat my wife with significance.* I was smart enough not to say these statements out loud!

The intent is to block out the sting of the criticism. They are justified in giving the criticism, but you need to diminish it while you are in the process of getting better.

To achieve my goal of being a better husband, I needed to block out another type of critic. This type of critic doesn't criticize with words, but rather enables by allowing me to be comfortable with not being a very good husband. Remember, sometimes your critics are more comfortable with you staying where you are.

Using Affirmative Reminders

Hans Goethe wrote, "Treat people as they are and they remain that way. Treat them as though they were what they are capable of becoming, and you will help them move toward and become like that which they are capable of becoming."

I love this quote and like to translate it this way:

If you see yourself where you are, then you will continue to be that way. The good news is you can mentally rehearse seeing yourself as you would like to be.

Remember, all meaningful, lasting change starts first in the imagination, then works its way out.

The key to forming new attitudes and habits is your self-talk. Every day you use your *words,* which trigger *pictures* that bring about *emotions.* You can design your self-talk with specific phrases or affirmative reminders that *trigger positive mental rehearsal that brings about the desired emotional impact to create new attitudes and habits.*

How do you move toward what you want to become or achieve?

Remember, the conscious mind selects only the information it considers important to be recorded into the subconscious mind. The goal is to get the correct information stored in your subconscious, because you are going to move toward and become like what you believe yourself to be (your self-image).

> *All meaningful, lasting change starts first in the imagination, then works its way out.*

Say you want to learn to take action rather than procrastinate. Procrastination is an attitude, a learned habit. What you can learn, you can unlearn. The key is using mental rehearsal to practice seeing yourself exactly as you want to become.

Flick Back and Flick Up

Affirmative reminders are an amazing technology for change. As you know, words trigger pictures, which create feelings or emotions. Affirmative reminders start the process of triggering positive images and generating the desired emotional impact.

Emotional impact is what brings the energy that leads to behavioral changes.

It isn't enough to just say the words. As I was working on being a better husband, I needed the help of emotion to cement that new attitude and behavior patterns. I visualized catching a winning touchdown, and I reflected on how it felt and how my teammates felt. With that feeling in place, I repeated to myself, *I love serving Cindy and treating her with significance.* I was tying that emotion of feeling like a winner to my thoughts of serving my wife. My brain then could apply that emotional energy to my new goal.

You need to visualize the pictures and images associated with the words you are saying and attach a positive feeling. Visualize doing it and explore and define the benefits of doing it. What are you going to get out of this when it happens? If you can't answer that question, there won't be any energy to fuel the change you are trying to create.

As a leader, it is important that you allow your employees to determine—and visualize—what is in it for them if a goal is reached. Again, it is what affects you emotionally that fuels the change, whether it is personal or professional change.

The key to forming new attitudes and habits is pretty simple. You have always talked to yourself, and whether you realized it or not, those words triggered pictures and certain emotions. Now, you can choose to design your self-talk with specific phrases, or affirmative reminders, that will trigger positive pictures.

Instead of the process working against you, it will work for you. Your words will bring about the desired emotional impact to create the attitudes and habits that you need to reach your goals.

Affirmative reminders allow you to visualize and experience the *future* as part of the *now*. As you state a new attitude, goal, or belief as if it's already been achieved, your mind allows you to feel it, sense it, and experience it. Time is collapsed.

Create your affirmative reminders and repeat them consistently for at least three to five weeks.

You will install your new thought pattern and self-image during that time, which will facilitate your new attitude and habit—a positive habit you can maintain.

For example, if your goal is to get in great shape, at the end of those five weeks, you will be mentally ready to exercise and eat right consistently. Remember, the ultimate results may take awhile. It might be six months to a year before you actually enjoy the benefits of being in great shape.

Just recently at the gym, someone asked me, "Eric tell me, how did you get so disciplined?"

"Well, I'm not really disciplined."

"What do you mean? You come to the gym every day."

"That's not discipline any more—it's habit. I used discipline to create that habit, but I no longer have to stay disciplined."

Do you see how this works? As soon as you create a habit and belief system, the hard part is over. *You* will simply act like *you*.

What affirmative reminders do you want to create? What affirmative reminders will collapse time and allow you to accomplish your goals?

This Is the Way I Am

Creating change can be difficult, right? Especially if you have been doing something a certain way for a very long time. It's like the rut of a marriage, getting in shape, or quitting smoking. It is normal to ask yourself, "Can I really break this habit or create long-lasting change?" Perhaps you have tried many times and been unsuccessful.

A long-term habit is something that you learned at one point and have been practicing for years.

Do you think you have been doing something the same way for twenty years? No, you have been doing this for one year twenty times! That's why it doesn't have to take you twenty years to break a habit you've had for twenty years. It may only take you three months to be free of it!

The MTG process not only frees such behavior but also gives you the keys to free your mind. As you learn the right mindset, it leads you to new behaviors and, as a result, new and improved results.

You can do this! With a small step in the right direction, you can achieve huge results.

Consistency is your secret sauce.

What is the worst thing that can happen if you create affirmative reminders and repeat them every day? If nothing happens, you've lost five minutes of your life per day for three weeks. A pretty small investment that could yield a huge return! Remember, this is about you. These five minutes a day are about goals that *you* want to accomplish. You have taken the time to stop and design what you want your life to look like.

Your assignment now is to write affirmative reminders as if they had already been accomplished. You could even take it to the next level and include pictures and illustrations.

As a leader, write an article like Howard Schultz and talk about how your organization is going to change the world.

I am not asking you to run wind sprints in the dead heat. You don't have to do laps or deadlifts. All I am asking you to do is write some things down and read them to yourself for five minutes every day!

Imagine what it is going to be like when your goals have actually been accomplished. That is the beginning. I am asking you to sign up and play. If you can't sign up for something this painless, I don't really have anything else for you.

One thing I can't remove from this process is your responsibility for making this change. It's up to you—100 percent. I am simply providing you the tools to be more effective as you take on this challenge.

Are you ready to take 100 percent responsibility for your results? Write your affirmative reminders and goals down. Your dreams for your life are worth recording. What do they look like? What is success for you?

Steps for Writing Affirmative Reminders

1. Personal: Write personally (include the word "I").
   You want *yourself (I)* to be an integral part of the affirmative reminder.

   Well-designed: *"I work with my goals in mind and plan ahead to get ahead."*

   Avoid comparisons with others. This is your personal program dealing with your thoughts, behaviors, relationships, and attitudes.

Well-designed: *"I am a well-prepared, goal-oriented, and people-minded leader, and it feels terrific."*

Affirmative reminders are to be selected, designed, and used by *you* on *you*. Put the responsibility on you to modify your behavior.

2. Positive: Envision what you want (state it positively and confidently).

   Describe what you want as opposed to what exists or what you do not want.

   Well-designed: *"I am an excellent speaker—well prepared, logical, and completely at ease with any group."*

3. Present: Write in the present tense ("I am").
   Clarity of behavior is important. Creating a clear picture of your desired behavior is more "impressive" to the subconscious mind than simply behaving somewhat better. Having reached this level of achievement is exciting for you. Express the affirmative reminder in the "now" as though it has already been achieved. Remember, the subconscious mind accepts information at face value. This dimension also has the effect of freeing you from mental blocks and conditioned limitations.

   Well-designed: *"I am an action person. I do first things first, one thing at a time, and follow through to a logical conclusion."*

   Words related to positive emotions create the most useful, vivid pictures.

   Well-designed: *"I am 100% accountable for my life and it feels incredible."*

4. Powerful: Use words that trigger positive emotions.
   Words related to positive emotions create the most useful, vivid pictures.

   Well-designed: *"I am 100 percent accountable for my life and it feels incredible."*

Particular: Use practical standards like "consistency" and "regularity." Avoid inflexible or perfect standards like "always" and "every time."

Well-designed: *"I regularly set a good example for people at work and at home."*

5. Precise: State specific desires and convictions.
   Wherever possible, use specific, measurable words.

Well-designed: *"I enjoy easily talking to ten new prospective customers weekly."*

When I played football, one of the phrases that I would use to spark emotion was, "I leave every drop of my blood on the field." It allowed me to create the picture and emotion that I needed to play with maximum effort.

Don't worry about being politically correct with your affirmative reminders. These statements are for you and you only. Use words that suggest constancy and regularity like "I am consistently…" Avoid words such as "always" or "every time." It just isn't realistic.

Lastly, state your specific desires. You don't walk into a restaurant and say, "I want some food." You ask for the specific item you want. This is the same concept.

Creating affirmative reminders certainly will help with your goal-setting, but it goes deeper than that: It helps you, teaches you, and trains you *how to live on purpose.*

As Zig Ziglar would say, "Don't become a wandering generality. Be a meaningful specific." Life is far better that way.

Some sample affirmative reminders are included in Appendix C at the back of the book. Make them your own and use them.

Regardless of whether you write your affirmative reminders from scratch or take them from a book or song, as long as they can help create the right picture in your mind, they are yours.

Earl Nightingale said it best: "What we do is we need to exchange a life of doubt, which is diversified or occasionally interrupted by faith, into a life of faith that is occasionally interrupted by doubt."

Affirmative reminders help you do just that.

Principles for Using Affirmative Reminders

1. Relax your body and mind.
    - You are not forcing this through willpower. It is the image that changes. Relax and go into the theater of your mind.

2. Review 3–5 times daily for 28–35 days.
    - Review your affirmative reminders when you wake up and when you go to bed. Also consider reviewing them when you are driving or in some other activity that requires less mental focus.

3. Use vivid, first-person imagery accompanied by emotion.
    - Imagine it in detail and feel what it would feel like to have what you are affirming. You might not realize this, but this works for you already. It's called worrying! Balance some of that worry with some positive expectations.

4. Hold the thought for 10–15 seconds.
    - Incorporate this short activity in your daily routine. Commit to visualizing your goals.

Vision of Success

You are establishing not only what you want your goals to look like, but what's even more important is what it will feel like. It's about seeing yourself there.

Visualization is daydreaming with a purpose.

My father would tell me, "Don't dress for the position you're in. Dress for the position you want to end up in." I'll never forget the first time that I bought a tie for about $50. I remember thinking, *What the heck? How in the world can any tie cost $50? I could get one for $7.* But Dad was right. It was all about what I felt like when I wore it.

When you visualize, you expand your comfort zone. As you imagine and feel your goals as already complete, ask yourself questions like:

How will I feel?

How does a person in this position behave?

How do they think?

Don't Stop Doing the Work

I have had setbacks and struggled during certain times. There have been countless moments when I wanted to throw in the towel and call it quits, but I knew that my challenges were providing the resistance and responsibility that my potential needed for it to be unleashed.

Our obstacles give us adventure! Without them, it would be like watching a movie with no ups or downs.

As you reflect on your previous failures and disappointments, it helps to ask yourself the right questions. Marcus Buckingham points out that we often ask ourselves the wrong questions when we reflect on past experiences. He states that we often ask, "What are the things that I need to remember or learn?" but the better question is, "What are the few things that I can never forget?"

Increasing your focus is a process of elimination, not addition.

Boil down to a few things in your life what will make the biggest difference. The content will change but not the process. The use of visualization, affirmative reminders, and positive self-talk will always be your tools, but what you use these tools on will change as you continue to narrow down on the key things that have the biggest impact for you and your future.

REFLECTIONS

- What you believe about yourself and the world around you is what you see.

- Your thoughts, beliefs, habits, and attitudes are all magnetic.

- An affirmative reminder is any new attitude, goal, or belief stated as though it has already been achieved.

- Flooding begins with changing your thoughts, as well as changing the images that lead to those thoughts.

- Your behaviors are simply beliefs acted upon.

- The "responsibility cycle for change" allows you to improve your performance by controlling your self-talk and redesigning the beliefs you hold in your subconscious mind.

- Your self-talk, ability to visualize, and the use of affirmative reminders are the tools that will influence and improve your self-image and self-esteem.

- There are three specific steps that you must do to elevate your self-image.
  - Monitor self-talk
  - Block out the critics
  - Imprint a new reality using affirmative reminders

- Steps for writing affirmative reminders:
  - Personal: Write personally
  - Positive: Envision what you want
  - Present: Write in the present tense
  - Powerful: Use words that trigger positive emotions
  - Particular: Use words that suggest consistency
  - Precise: State specific desires and convictions
  - Visualization is daydreaming with a purpose.

10

YOUR PERSONAL GAME PLAN

Small Actions, Big Results

It's time to bring it all together and create your personal game plan. You have learned an incredible amount in the last nine chapters, so the goal now is to take all this great information and narrow it down to small actions that lead to big results.

Someone once taught me how powerful the small act of smiling could be. He challenged me to smile genuinely at as many people as I could for one entire day and observe their reactions. What a great idea! It was amazing how many people smiled back and how many conversations began. I experienced exceptional customer service at every business establishment. It seemed as if each person I ran into was having the best day ever. I even smiled while talking to colleagues on the phone and listened to their words, tone, and inflection be extremely positive. A smile was such a small simple action, but it created huge results!

In this final chapter, you will learn how to use the affirmative reminder process to create a unique and powerful *plan of action* to clarify your goals and take small actions to set them into motion.

Personal strategic planning begins from the inside out and starts with small steps. As you create your plan of action, the intent is to break your dream down into small chunks to make it more manageable.

A good friend of mine, Erik Van Alstine, stated it isn't that your dream is too big, but if you take too big a bite, you can choke on it.

You need to take small bites, to enjoy the eating experience, and not attempt to eat a whole cake in one sitting!

Big goal, small steps—that is what makes all the difference.

These small actions will lead to big results, but it is important that you take small action steps every single day. This technique is called "continuous action technique" (CAT). Create a to-do list by asking yourself, "What can I do today that moves me toward my goal?"

Keep in mind, *this isn't a chore list!* A chore is something you have to do that often you just want to be done with. This is different—making efforts toward your goals is an adventure, a journey to achieving your long-held desires in life!

It has been said, "You can't cross a sea by merely staring into the water." Make time to take action, regardless of how small.

> *Do not despise small beginnings...*
> —Zechariah 4:10

Think about WIN—What's Important Now?

Winning is simply knowing and doing what's important now (WIN). Coaches encourage their teams to "win" this moment and win this play...then do it again. They win the game by winning one play at a time.

Because it takes time for your small actions to build and gain momentum toward your goals, you must maintain perspective and realize that each action is like a small investment—in yourself and your dreams.

Would you rather have $1 million cash or a penny that doubles in value every day for 31 days?

When I ask this question of my audiences, the typical response is, "I will take the $1 million!"

"Are you sure you want the $1 million?" I ask.

"I am sure!"

My audience chooses the $1 million, and I take the penny that doubles. The audience members are instant hypothetical millionaires and after ten days, I have a whopping $5.12.

After twenty days, the audience still has their $1 million, and I have a grand total of $5,243.00. Looks like the audience made the right choice, doesn't it?

Not so fast, after twenty-eight days that penny is now worth $1,342,177.28!

"Now how do you feel about your choice?" I ask the audience.

"Pretty good, because you only have a few hundred thousand dollars more than we do," they defensively respond.

"Okay, but let's look at day 29. My money doubles again to $2,684,354.56. On day 30, it doubles again to $5,368,709.12 and on day 31, it doubles again for a grand total of $10,737,418.24!

Now, how do you feel about choosing the $1 million over the penny that doubles every day for 31 days?"

"Not so good," they reply.

I want you to think about what you want. Instead of a magic penny that compounds daily, I want you to think of small acts you can do that will have a compounding effect on the important areas of your life.

The accomplishment of your goals may take longer than thirty-one days, but the small acts of reviewing and visualizing your goals continuously will have a similar compounding effect.

There will be sacrifices along the way. It can be hard to keep going when you still are eating Top Ramen and you see others eating steak who opted to "take the $1 million versus the compounding penny."

> *You do not necessarily reach your goals through brilliance; you reach your goals through continuance.*

Remember, as you progress toward your goal, there will be times that you see very little progress being made. You do not necessarily reach your goals through brilliance; you reach your goals through continuance. *Failure* is the path of least resistance.

This is why you continue to build a healthy self-image and maintain high self-esteem in order to overcome the challenges that you will face while pursuing your goal. By following the MTG principles and creating a plan of action, you are planting the right seeds and growing the right roots to accomplish your goals. But you must be intentional.

Let's create your plan of action.

Develop a Plan of Action

1. Identify your breakthrough goal.
2. Clarify the benefits.
3. Identify the obstacles you can control.
4. Define the solutions to those obstacles.
5. Rewrite the goal as an affirmative reminder.
6. Rewrite the solution as affirmative reminders.
7. Transfer your plan of action to a 3x5 card, smartphone, etc.
8. Breakthrough goal

In Chapter Eight, you began to think about and write down your goals. It is now time to identify your breakthrough goal. Your breakthrough goal is the goal that *elevates* all your other goals. Here are some questions to help you identify your breakthrough goal:

- From your list of goals, which goal, when accomplished, would have the most significant impact on your life right now?
- Which goal excites you the most and would enable you to add the most value to your family, company, etc.?
- If you could accomplish only one goal from your list, what goal would that be?

Make sure your goal is a big deal to you and, when accomplished, is a big deal to those around you.

I define goal-setting as painting a picture of your desired future. That does not mean your picture of the future must be a self-portrait. It is highly motivating when you think of the positive impact your goal will have on the lives of others when it is accomplished.

> *Every great accomplishment was once an impossibility.*
> —Unknown

I have spent a lot of time with a friend who served many years in the special forces of the U.S. military. He had been in over 1,000 firefights—literally bullets flying past his head over 1,000 times! He had been deployed to various countries eighteen times. On many of these assignments, his wife had no clue when he would leave—or return. He had been to Afghanistan, Iraq (Fallujah), and the Philippines, to name a few.

Obviously, there were many details of his missions he couldn't talk about, but there was one thing he said that really stuck with me. He talked about how important his *mindset* was during the mission. He was involved in some very dangerous, significant situations, but he still had to focus on the details. If he allowed himself to be distracted by the weight of the mission, he could possibly miss an important detail that could have terrible consequences.

Instead of allowing the weight of the mission to distract him, he used the weight of the mission to focus on the small details that make a big difference.

His self-talk was, "Each time I focus and complete a small action, I am fulfilling the mission." He thought of his family, the families of his peers, and all the servicemen and women who came before him. He reminded himself that he was part of something bigger than himself.

What you are pursuing has to be significant enough for you to willingly pay the price.

It wasn't during conflict that he needed more motivation. He needed it for the daily monotonous detail work that was also critical to the mission.

In the NFL, there is a mantra among the players and coaches that states, "We are paid to practice, and we play for free!" Finding the motivation to play on game day in front of 80,000 fans in the stadium and millions of viewers on digital platforms is easy. Finding the drive to practice day in and day out without an audience is what separates the good players from the great players, the good teams from the great teams.

What you are pursuing has to be significant enough for you to willingly pay the price.

What you do when no one is looking will dictate what you do when everyone is looking.

Winners are made in the dark...celebrated in the light.
—Unknown

Clarify the Benefits

You have identified your breakthrough goal, so the next step is to clarify the benefits.

What are the benefits for you moving toward and accomplishing the goal?

The benefits are the "whys" behind your goal. The longer your list, the stronger your motivation. Instead of using willpower to reach your goals, use "why-power" to reach your goals.

Answer these questions:

- Why do you want to achieve this breakthrough goal?
- What will you miss out on if you don't accomplish your goal?
- What pain will you experience as a result of not accomplishing your goal?
- What great things will you gain as a result of reaching this goal?

Think about it and list every single reason that comes to mind. For example, if your goal is to earn $1 million, you need to ask yourself, "Why do I *really* want to earn that?" What you may discover is that your goal isn't really to earn $1 million. Maybe you want to live like a millionaire, but not pay taxes like a millionaire.

There might be many ways to accomplish your goal, but until you start writing out the reasons and the whys, you won't obtain the clarity that you need to accomplish it.

Reasons come first. Answers come second.

It is critical that you understand the power that is created with clarifying your whys. It's effective not only in goal-setting, but also in everything that you do.

When you are changing an attitude or habit or pursuing a tangible goal, you need to feed and strengthen your reasons as to why this change will make a difference in your life. You have to fuel your "fire of desire."

There are two competing emotions we deal with on a regular basis: fear and desire. The emotion that wins is the emotion you feed the most. When you list the whys for your pursued goal, it feeds your desire. The longer and stronger your list of whys, the stronger your desire.

As I have said previously, *keep your fire of desire burning hot!*

As a leader, it is also important to clarify the "why" with your team.

Why is accomplishing this goal or performance metric important? What is in it for you? What is in it for your team? Define whether the goal has an emotional reward, a financial reward, or a future opportunity reward. The reasons are the kindling to your fire.

As you answer these questions for yourself, you also give the opportunity for your employees or team members to answer the same questions.

- What's in it for them?
- Why is the goal important for them?
- What is the benefit?

Resist the temptation to identify the benefits and the "whys" for your team. Allow them to identify the benefits for themselves.

More often than not, the benefits that you identify for yourself are never the same benefits that your employees or team members identify. If you try to impose your identified benefits on them, you will automatically create resentment and resistance.

Identify the Obstacles

*What are the obstacles that **you can control** that keep you from moving toward the goal?*

Notice the keywords in that question. I want you to focus on obstacles that are in the realm of your control. What are the things that you are or are not doing that impede your progress?

As you reflect on possible obstacles, move from a state of mind that focuses on feelings to actual behaviors. For example, if the fear of rejection is an obstacle, what do you actually *do or fail to do* as a result of your fear of rejection? By focusing on actual behaviors, the obstacles become much more concrete and practical, and you can uncover specific solutions. Do you see the difference?

When working with teams, I sometimes hear that an obstacle is a lack of trust, but the real obstacle is what the team is or isn't doing as *a result of* a lack of trust. It is important to drill down to the actual behavior. Team members may be having side conversations instead of talking about the real problem in the initial meeting. They aren't going directly to the source and talking about the specific behavior.

By asking the right questions and tackling these obstacles from an actual behavior mindset, you can effectively solve these complex issues within the team—and build trust.

We all experience factors that are out of our control, but you don't want to waste your energy, time, or money on things that you can't influence. That is why it is necessary to have this filter. If you focus on what you can control, you will uncover what the primary obstacles are.

Once you start identifying the obstacles, you will realize that not all of them carry equal weight. Some are more impactful than others.

What obstacles will make it *most difficult* for you to accomplish your goal?

Define the Solutions

What are possible solutions to the obstacles that you have control over? Be as *specific* as possible. They must be solutions that are actionable—in other words, something that you can do something with. Make an effort to focus on solutions that get to the few things that actually matter the most.

> *What are possible solutions to the obstacles that you have control over? Be as specific as possible.*

To illustrate this, a high school in my area was having an issue with students being late to class throughout the day. Teachers were frustrated because they had to wait until the halls were empty to start class. Instead of implementing a solution of punishment and discipline, they decided to drill down deeper and brainstorm possible reasons why a significant number of students were late to class.

The administration was willing to ask some exploratory questions of the students and of themselves. Do the students have enough time between classes? What is preventing them from being on time? What if we were to allow a few more minutes?

These questions allowed the administrators to find an actionable solution that would have the most impact. They did end up extending the time between classes, which made it easier for the students to arrive on time.

William of Ockham (1287–1347), a British philosopher, believed, "The simplest and most direct solution requiring the fewest number of steps is usually the correct solution to any problem." William's method of problem solving was widely accepted by the scientific community and is still known today as Occam's Razor.

Far too often we allow problem solving to become overly complicated. This occurs when the solution challenges us to face our fears.

Write down the actionable solutions that you identify for your obstacles.

Write the Goal as an Affirmative Reminder

Now go back to the goal and rewrite it as though you have already accomplished it.

Write your breakthrough goal as an affirmative reminder and do it in a way that visually brings the goal to life.

As I began my speaking and consulting career, I took a similar approach. When people look at my background, their first reaction is, "Oh, you are a sports guy," but rarely is a "sports guy" sitting in front of a boardroom talking strategy in a business setting. If someone had looked at my resume before I began my speaking and consulting career, there was nothing there that screamed management consul-

> *I had a powerful affirmative reminder describing my breakthrough goal as if it had already taken place.*

tant expert. I had played and coached football, asked a lot of questions of coaches along the way, watched how things worked in churches and other nonprofit agencies, and tried to apply some of the information I'd learned. None of this actually qualified me to become a management consulting expert.

My breakthrough goal was to be an international leadership consultant, keynote speaker, and executive coach. My goal actually came from reading someone else's bio, and I just substituted my name. I didn't exactly know how to accomplish my dream at the time, but I had a powerful affirmative reminder describing my breakthrough goal as if it had already taken place.

My breakthrough goal written as an affirmative reminder:

I travel the world coaching, training, and inspiring leaders to unleash their potential and the potential of those they serve.

Writing down your breakthrough goal as an affirmative reminder creates amazing results. It allows you to get a clear view (to the best of your ability) of what your accomplished goal is going to look and feel like.

Write the Solutions as Affirmative Reminders

Do the very same thing that you just did with your breakthrough goal.

Restate the possible solutions that you previously defined as positive, present-tense affirmative reminders.

Let me illustrate this. After I defined my breakthrough goal of being an international consulting executive coach and best-selling author, I identified obstacles and possible solutions to those obstacles.

One of my solutions was that I had to talk, walk, listen, and function as if I belonged on stage as well as in the boardroom. This was quite a stretch for me, because when I created my goal, my inside voice was screaming, "Intruder! Intruder! Who do you think you are?"

At the time, even though I had made it to the NFL and accomplished something that less than 0.001 percent of the population could do, I saw myself as a failure. I lacked self-worth and confidence. I needed an affirmative reminder to build those things.

For my solution, I wrote a supportive affirmative reminder as follows:

I'm calm, cool, and collected in every environment that I'm in. I do first things first, one thing at a time. Follow through always. I am always discovering the small thing that makes the biggest difference. I am courageous and confident while asking questions that no one else is willing to ask.

I created affirmative reminders that helped me become as comfortable as possible in my own skin, so that when I was in environments where others wouldn't speak up, I would. I read my affirmative reminders every morning and every night, consistently, every day. I didn't believe what I was reading at first, but I was growing my belief by constantly reading day after day.

Belief is a process that is built on repetition. It was amazing how that single affirmative reminder had such a positive impact on my performance and ability to be in this new environment.

Today, I am able to give counsel with confidence and help the executives I'm coaching process their situation to ensure they achieve their goal. Stating your solutions as affirmative reminders adds fuel to your bonfire and gives you a burning desire to take actions that lead to your breakthrough goal.

> *When I created my goal, my inside voice was screaming, "Intruder! Intruder! Who do you think you are?"*

Becomes an Expectation

Now that you have developed your plan of action, transfer it to a 3x5 card so that you can easily review it every single day. Remember, it is that daily review that allows your new self to emerge and accomplish your goal. Your breakthrough goal started as a hope. Through the MTG process that hope grows into a belief, and that belief becomes an expectation. As soon as it becomes an expectation, you take action on your goal.

You expect, therefore you act. When your goal is now an expectation, your mindset changes.

You don't feel the same level of discomfort when you say it, neither does it feel like it is too far out that it has no impact. If your goal is too far out of your realm, you can't even picture what it even means. But now, because your goal is an expectation not only can you feel it, but you feel a sense of disappointment and loss if it doesn't happen. This loss aversion means you feel like this goal *belongs* to you. It is yours. When that occurs, you have shifted from hoping for something to really *expecting* it to happen.

Grow Your Roots

To accomplish our goals, the growth of a Chinese bamboo tree teaches us the importance of faith, persistence, and, most importantly, changing from the inside out.

When you plant the seed of a Chinese bamboo tree, you go through an entire growing season without seeing anything. You continue to water and nurture the soil, but there is no evidence of anything coming out of the ground. In fact, it is necessary to put a mark in the ground where you planted the seed so that you know the location.

The second growing season comes and goes. Still nothing. The third, nothing. There is still no evidence of your Chinese bamboo tree.

Finally, the fourth growing season comes, and you probably are ready to give up and quit. You get down on your hands and knees and look closely at the mark in the ground—still nothing! You wonder if the time and energy and resources you are putting into this seed year after year is worth it. Are you wasting your time?

You decide to give it one more year.

During the fifth growing season, something unique happens. All of a sudden, not only does the Chinese bamboo tree come out of the ground, it grows up to eighty feet high in one growing season! To any outsiders looking on, this appears to be a miracle that happened overnight. But if you planted the seed and know how much work, patience, and diligence it took for five-plus years to get that tree to grow, you understand how long the "miracle" took. The visible bamboo tree grew in a hurry, but not necessarily overnight. For the first five years, all the growth occurred beneath the surface. The root structure was taking shape and preparing itself for the upward growth.

If you could see it, the root structure of a Chinese bamboo—if stretched out in a line—would extend for miles. It is strong and intricate as it creates a web of roots deep into the earth's soil.

The transformation of your goals is going to happen the same way. The change happens on the inside, beneath the surface where you can't see it. And it probably will take nurturing over some significant time.

As you focus your attention on positive self-talk, use affirmations, work hard, and visualize your goals, you are growing the root structure in the soil of your mind that is necessary for your goals to become a reality.

Don't give up! Know that your hard work and persistence are growing the roots. Even though you don't see the evidence yet with your physical eyes, you can still see it in your mind's eye. All will come into focus as you change from the inside out.

Celebrate Your Wins

As you embark on this journey of unleashing your potential, it is important to celebrate and acknowledge your wins along the way.

Keeping a daily win journal is another tool of success that has a powerful influence on your ability to achieve your goals.

It is important to not only capture life's moments but also to recreate the intensity of those moments. The way you do that is by reflecting on them. By acknowledging your wins, not only do you make progress toward your goal, but you also strengthen your emotional immune system for any negativity that might come your way.

A happy, fulfilling life is not a life absent of problems and challenges. We must recognize and celebrate joy and happiness among our problems and challenges. As Maxwell Maltz stated, "Happiness is a state of mind where one's thoughts are pleasant the majority of the time." Capturing daily wins, no matter how small, prevents the 10 percent of your life that may not be right to control 100 percent of your thinking.

One of my late dear friends, Kit Taylor, was an inspired practitioner of celebrating his wins. I met Kit at Aviva, one of the companies that implemented the Moving to Great change management process. Kit was a certified MTG Master Facilitator and trained thousands of colleagues in the MTG principles.

I showed him my daily win journal, and he embraced the practice immediately. The next day he showed up with his own win journal and from that day forward, he wrote down every win that happened in his life. He also included his affirmative reminders and his goals.

Some of the critical areas that Kit identified were his relationships with his wife, Sarah, and children, Harry, Millie, and Alice, and the impact he wanted to have on them. Kit's particular breakthrough goal was his relationship and mission with Sarah. One of Kit's affirmative reminders read, "I renew my vows and recommit my love to my wife Sarah every day. She is the most important thing in my life."

Kit was 100 percent committed to this practice. He constantly communicated and demonstrated his love for his wife and kids with text messages, notes, and spending time with them. They knew that Kit loved them. In fact, one night when Kit was working late away from home, he got a text from his wife: "What are you doing?"

"I'm still in the office. I'm getting ready to go. Where are you at?"

She mentioned a certain store.

"There's no store like that in our town."

"I know. I am here in town."

She had driven three hours just to have dinner with him that night! That was when he knew that what he was doing was significant. They had built an amazing relationship.

When Kit and I would touch base, he always would express his excitement for his goals and family. He would tell me, "Eric, the more I review my wins and affirmative reminders, the more I appreciate my wife and family. My appreciation grows the more I focus on it. As I write how special she is, every day I see more reasons why she is special."

Kit inspired me incredibly, both personally and professionally. He illustrated the realness and the power of focusing on your daily wins and building on them. From him I learned firsthand how to make sure my wife and family felt significant and loved. I began the practice of sending messages to my wife, Cindy, and my daughters, Taylor and Madison.

After he completed the Moving to Great training, the messages that he started getting from colleagues throughout his whole organization were amazing. Talk about a guy who lived the MTG principles!

When I saw Kit for the last time, he had lost thirty pounds, was in the best shape of his life, and his countenance was so bright! The MTG principles had enabled Kit to focus on the things that really mattered to him. Kit's breakthrough goal—his relationship and mission with his wife—had improved and impacted every area of his life. He had correctly identified his breakthrough goal, because it was the one thing that made all of his other goals come into alignment.

MTG changed the way he parented and the way he dealt with people. Everything changed. With his boundless energy, he was very clear on what he wanted and how to go about getting it. When I learned of Kit's passing due to a heart condition, I was completely devastated. I spent the majority of the day reminiscing with his family, friends, and colleagues and sharing some of our fondest memories through laughter and tears. Kit's spirit will live on in his amazing family, as well as in the hearts and minds of the people who study and apply the Moving to Great principles.

I am confident that you too will experience the great levels of success that Kit and the millions of other inspired MTG practitioners have experienced!

> *Somebody should tell us right at the start of our lives that we are dying. Then we might live life to the limit, every minute of every day. Do it! I say. Whatever you want to do, do it now! There are only so many tomorrows.*
>
> —Michael Landon

My mentor, Bob Moawad, said it best: "My desire for you is that the best of your past will become the worst of your future from now on."

The best is yet to come.

REFLECTIONS

- Think about WIN—What's Important Now.

- Develop a plan of action.
  - Identify the breakthrough goal.
  - Clarify the benefits.
  - Identify the obstacles you can control.
  - Define the solutions to those obstacles.
  - Rewrite the goal as an affirmative reminder.
  - Rewrite the solution as affirmative reminders.
  - Transfer your plan of action to a 3x5 card, smartphone, etc.

- Every great accomplishment was once an impossibility.

- What you do when no one is looking dictates what you do when everyone is looking.

- Reasons come first. Answers come second.

- Define possible solutions to the obstacles that you have control over. Be as *specific* as possible.

- "The simplest and most direct solution requiring the fewest number of steps is usually the correct solution to any problem."—William of Ockham, a British philosopher (1287–1347)

- Write your breakthrough goal as an affirmative reminder and do it in a way that visually brings the goal to life.

- Restate the possible solutions that you previously defined as positive, present-tense affirmative reminders.

- Keeping a daily win journal is another tool of success that has a powerful influence on your ability to achieve your goals.

SELF-DISCOVERY QUESTIONS

1. Breakthrough goal: Which one of your goals, when accomplished, would have the most significant impact on your life right now?
2. What are the benefits for you of moving toward and accomplishing the goal?
3. What are the obstacles that *you can control* that keep you from moving toward the goal?

CONCLUSION

Motivation gets you going, but *discipline* keeps you growing," said John Maxwell. Your challenge is to discipline yourself and develop a laser-like focus on your own individual growth.

My whole story began with a dream. I began my executive coaching career speaking to my youth basketball team of eight-year-old boys. As I delivered my pre-game and post-game speeches, I would pretend that I was speaking to a group of executives, vice presidents, and leaders—and some of those boys actually have grown into these roles—but what it did for me was allow me to practice and visualize where I one day wanted to end up.

Fast forward a few years...I am walking the streets of London in the business section not too far from Buckingham Palace. I meet with the leadership team of one of the largest global banks in the world. I sit in the executive boardroom with the CEO and various leaders who graduated from highly esteemed institutions such as Oxford University and Cambridge University. One of the gentlemen asks me, "How did you get started executive coaching?"

"I coached a youth basketball team," I reply.

Not satisfied with my answer, he asks, "Okay, but how did you get from there to here, sitting in this room? What changed?"

"I did."

The most important thing that changed was *me*.

Moving to Great is all about getting you from here to there.

My goal is to inspire you to create a bigger *there* and take action growing yourself. Be willing to ask yourself, "What can I do, where can I go, and how can I get better?" When you change yourself, everything around you changes. Your power, control, and influence are within. This is the MTG way, and this is where the hope is.

You don't have to depend on anyone else to accomplish your goals. Your success doesn't depend on anyone outside yourself. It depends on you, and you now know how to unleash the potential that is lying dormant.

I know these principles work. I practice them every day. They work personally as well as professionally. You *can* accomplish your goals—it is just a matter of which ones you want to focus on. You must focus, demonstrate discipline, and be willing to work through the MTG process.

Along the way, I encourage you to share your wins with as many people as you can. We all need hope, and hope comes from seeing each other be successful when dealing with life's challenges.

Establish a success partner and share your wins with each other. Be each other's cheerleader. Also, commit to a daily routine of making time for yourself and your goals. Start with ten to fifteen minutes in the morning and at night. As you gain momentum and create a habit, increase the amount of time.

In the morning, feed yourself mentally and spiritually. Read a good book, meditate, or do something that makes you feel good. Review and visualize your goals and desires.

To finish your day well, no matter what happened, it is important to capture your wins and specifically identify what inspires your gratefulness before you go to sleep. Ask yourself, "What do I want to remember about today?" We choose our memories consciously, so decide to remember the good things.

As you do these things daily and follow the principles in this book, you will realize that you didn't reach your goals, but rather your goals *reached you.*

Goal attainment isn't an event, it's a lifestyle—a continual movement toward bigger and better things.

Fall in love with the process. I invite you to reach out and share with me your wins, thoughts, or comments. I believe in the power of the MTG principles, and I believe in you.

As my mentor once told me, may the best of your past become the worst of your future.

God bless.

ACKNOWLEDGMENTS

Writing a book is a team sport, and there are many to thank. First, my wife of twenty years, Cindy, for your unwavering belief in me. *Moving to Great* exists today because of your unconditional love and support. I love you.

To my daughters, Taylor and Madison, I am the proudest dad in the world. I love you so much. Thank you for your constant encouragement and for allowing me to practice these tools and techniques on you without complaining too much.

To my biggest fan: my mother, Cathy Boles, thank you for loving me unconditionally. You have been such a blessing to me all my life, and this book is just as much your work as it is mine. To both my fathers, the late J.A. Boles Sr. and Cicero Bess, thank you for all your years of wisdom and guidance. To my extended family, thank you for your prayers and support.

Moving to Great wouldn't be great at all without my editorial team. First, Bruce Nygren, for making the words work just right, and Cory Emberson, for the thousand fixes you made in the final work. Thank you, Rebekah Harkness, for your tireless effort in helping me get these ideas onto paper. Your professionalism and commitment are second to none. Erik and Sandra at Stone Lounge Press, thank you for orchestrating it all.

Thank you to my team at The Game Changers. Christy Magana, thank for managing this project with excellence. This book could not have been done without you. Thank you, Diane Vaccaro, for managing our business and ensuring we serve our clients with integrity. Thank you, Larry Hultz, for your commitment to us sharing these principles all over the world.

To my covenant group—Jon Kitna, Sean McKay, and Travis Brown—thank you for sharpening me and making sure my walk matches my talk. As it says in Proverbs 27:17, "As iron sharpens iron, so one man sharpens another."

To those whose mentorship and influence changed my life, your work lives on in my own. My mentors include the late Bob Moawad Sr., Richard (Dick) Anderson, the late Dr. Ken Hutcherson, Scotty Kessler, the late Frosty Westering, the late Mike Dunbar, Mike Holmgren, Andy Reid, Pete Carroll, Bobby Ross, Gil Byrd, John Anderson, Norm LeMay, the late Charles Mitchell, Mother Sara Turner, Rosa Cartledge, the late Lillie Green, Allen Jones, Dean and Anne Curry, and many more.

Finally, to the more than a quarter million people around the world that I've had the privilege to coach, teach, and inspire, thank you for inspiring me. The experts say no book is perfect, but I pray this book is perfect for you.

About the Author

Eric Boles is the president of The Game Changers, Inc., a training and development company that helps companies achieve goals quickly and work in alignment with their purposes and values. In that role, Eric is a highly acclaimed keynote speaker and consultant for some of the most recognized and respected organizations in the world, including Starbucks, UPS, SAP, Michelin, Motorola, Swiss Re, MGM, Aviva, Alaska Airlines, and the U.S. Air Force. He's also an avid sports fan, golfer, and reader. He and his wife, Cindy, have two daughters and live in the Seattle area.

Appendix A

JOURNEY OF AWARENESS

Thousands of participants have told me that expanding their awareness has been personally profitable to them, and I know it will have similar value to you.

Your actions and decisions are based on your current level of awareness. To better understand this, it is necessary to do a personal awareness inventory of yourself as you are *right now* in your life. These questions serve as a personal awareness inventory, an honest and exhaustive consideration of both assets and liabilities. These questions allow you to take a strong first step toward getting better and becoming what you are capable of becoming.

My Awareness of Self

1. Identify a major challenge in your life and apply the following questions to it.
   a. Where have I shortchanged myself through a lack of honesty?
   b. Have I faced my challenge, or have I sidestepped it through daydreaming, wishful thinking, resentments, and self-pity? Explain.

2. What are some areas of my life where I have been saying, "I can't take this anymore" and am now willing to say, "I can take this and a lot more"?

My Awareness of My Family

1. What do I do to work at consistently gaining and keeping the love and respect of my spouse, children, parents, and siblings?
2. How do I demonstrate my love and respect for them by examples and actions?
3. What areas of my behavior would I like to change or improve regarding my family?
4. What qualities of mine do I want my children to have?

My Awareness of My Work

1. Who do I know that I would like to change jobs with? Why?
2. What work habits do I have that I would want someone working for me to have?
3. What work habits do I have that I would *not* want someone working for me to have?
4. What goals do I have to ensure my production level is at its highest?
5. What do I contribute to create a positive work atmosphere for myself and my fellow employees?
6. How much money is necessary for me? How many hours a week do I want to work?
7. In what ways do I live up to the standards that I expect of others?
8. What, if any, are the ethical considerations in my work that clash with my moral standards? How do I justify these areas of conflict?

My Awareness of My Friends, Neighbors, and Community

1. Why do I cultivate friendship?
2. What do I expect to receive from my friends? Do they owe me anything?
3. How do I express interest in my neighbors and their families?

Appendix B

SELF-IMAGE SURVEY

Your self-image is a complex picture of what you believe you are capable of, who you believe you are, and what you believe you deserve. It controls your thoughts, habits, and attitude. Located in your subconscious mind, it impacts your belief system about yourself and the world around you.

Your self-image is your performance regulator. Your self-image is an internal psychological thermostat that regulates your level of performance as well as your comfort zones. Your self-image doesn't define your potential, but it can *limit* your potential.

Because you will never consistently perform higher than your current self-image, it is important to explore it and identify the beliefs about yourself that are limiting your potential. Take this survey below to identify the susceptibilities in your self-image and create affirmations to attack your false and self-destructive beliefs.

Score as follows:
3	True
2	Mostly True
1	Somewhat True
0	Not True

Are there statements where you scored a "0" or "1" where you would like to change your image? Put a check mark next to them, and use the MTG principles to change your self-image in these areas.

Points		Statement of Present Action or Condition
_____	1.	I do not belittle, criticize, or condemn other people.
_____	2	I feel warm and good about myself all the time.
_____	3.	I am free of resentment and hostility.
_____	4.	I am not afraid of others' opinions and attitudes.
_____	5.	I do not withhold my needs, opinions, or feelings to please others.
_____	6.	I freely express my emotions.
_____	7.	I live up to and fulfill all my commitments—to self and others.
_____	8.	I am kind, gentle, and patient with myself.
_____	9.	I accept the responsibility for my life and direct it constructively.
_____	10.	I readily make prompt decisions and accept the consequences.
_____	11.	I do not blame others for my mistakes or problems.
_____	12.	I face reality and truths that can't be quickly changed.
_____	13.	I am the final authority for all that I do.
_____	14.	I analyze and change to benefit from my mistakes.
_____	15.	I allow myself to do my own thinking.
_____	16.	I express and stand up for my convictions and opinions.
_____	17.	I do not accept the put-downs and insults of others.
_____	18.	I control my self-talk and do not belittle or devalue myself.
_____	19.	I get satisfaction from doing my job well.
_____	20.	I do not normally look to others for support.
_____	21.	I accept problems as a challenge to my creativity.
_____	22.	I do not need others' approval or agreement to do as I see fit.
_____	23.	I do not impose my values and opinions on others.
_____	24.	I am not affected by comparisons to others.
_____	25.	I do not let people talk me into situations against my judgment.
_____	26.	I do not attempt to prove my worth through my accomplishments.
_____	27.	I always treat everyone with respect and consideration.
_____	28.	I do not attempt to make myself "right" and others "wrong."
_____	29.	I easily take the initiative in personal relationships.
_____	30.	I am free of all pretensions and open with everyone.
_____		TOTAL

Appendix C

SAMPLE AFFIRMATIVE REMINDERS

An affirmative reminder is any new attitude, goal, or belief stated as though it has already been achieved. Affirmative reminders are an excellent tool to update your mind with a new blueprint. They improve your self-image and self-esteem by imprinting your goals into your subconscious mind and belief system.

Affirmative reminders start the process of triggering positive images and generating the desired emotional impact. They allow you to visualize and experience the future as part of the now. As you state a new attitude, goal, or belief as though it has already been achieved, you feel it, sense it, and experience it. An affirmative reminder collapses time.

Below are some sample affirmative reminders. Identify which ones you could benefit from the most, based on your goals and values. Tweak them as necessary. Most importantly, repeat them multiple times every day for at least three to five weeks. They will strengthen your self-image and move you closer to your desired outcome and goals.

- I feel calm and patient with those who see things differently than I do.
- I enjoy creating a warm, positive, and loving home environment.
- I feel excitement when exciting people are around me.
- I use my utmost potential and feel fulfilled and happy.

- I have an excellent, free-flowing memory with clear and easy recall.
- I enjoy setting a good example for people at work and at home.
- I demonstrate my feelings of happiness by easily wearing a warm smile and sharing it with others.
- I consistently plan my work and follow through on my plans.
- I enjoy treating people as though they were what they want to be and helping them become what they are capable of becoming.
- I treat problems as opportunities to be creative and thus lead a fulfilled life.
- I am calm, poised, cool, and collected in pressure situations.
- I have high energy and enjoy being a self-starter.
- I am an excellent speaker. I am prepared, logical, and I love to share my insights with others.
- I am honest with myself and others, and this makes me feel great.
- I take accountability for all my actions. I feel dignity and pride in doing so.
- I enjoy having an abundant supply of energy and draw upon it for each task I choose to do.
- I enjoy sustaining my energy with healthy choices— in diet, exercise, rest, and relationships.
- I am very flexible and respond comfortably to change.